D1625010

Growing Hybrid Orchids Indoors

Growing Hybrid Orchids Indoors

Jack Kramer

UNIVERSE BOOKS
New York

All of the drawings in *Growing Hybrid Orchids Indoors* were
published previously in *Miniature Orchids to Grow and Show*
by Jack Kramer and Roy Crafton (New York: Norton,
1981).

Published in the United States of America in 1985
by Universe Books
381 Park Avenue South, New York, N.Y. 10016

85 86 87 88 89 / 10 9 8 7 6 5 4 3 2 1

Printed in the United States of America

Library of Congress Cataloging in Publication Data

Kramer, Jack, 1927-
    Growing hybrid orchids indoors.

    Bibliography: p.
    Includes index.
    1. Orchid culture. 2. Orchids. I. Title.
II. Title: Hybrid orchids at home.
SB409.K69 1985   635.9′3415   84-24088
ISBN 0-87663-392-0

Contents

Acknowledgments

Through the years I have been in contact with almost all of the mail-order suppliers of orchids in the United States, and general thanks go to those fine companies, but in particular I want to express my gratitude and appreciation for information, questions answered, and photographs to the following: Gene Hausermann of Hausermann Orchids; Hermann Pigors of Oak Hill Gardens; Frank Shride of Beall Orchids; Warren Kelly of Orchid World International Inc.; Robert Jones of Mt. Madonna Orchids; and Robert Westcott of Westcott Orchids.

Lists of orchid suppliers are found in the appendices at the back of this book.

And, as always, my grateful thanks and appreciation to the American Orchid Society, 6000 South Olive Avenue, West Palm Beach, Florida 33405.

Preface

Orchids were first used for medicinal purposes, as were many other plants of ancient times. Because the bulbs of many orchids are shaped like testicles, it was assumed that certain orchid roots or tubers, when boiled and eaten, were aphrodisiacs. In 1640, John Parkinson, a London apothecary and royal herbalist for Charles I, said that orchids, which he called *Cynsorchis*, stimulated lust. At that time, people believed that plants exercised powers over the welfare of human beings because certain leaves, flowers, and seeds resembled parts of the human anatomy. Thus, if a plant's leaf resembled a human liver, the plant was obviously intended as a remedy for hepatic disease. Similarly, a heart-shaped flower should cure cardiac ailments. Not until the 18th century was botanical science born and the first attempts at plant classification made. In 1794, there were fifteen different epiphytic orchids in the Royal Botanic Gardens of Kew, near London.

The start of the 1800s heralded a mania for gardening in England, and plants—all kinds—became a way of life for the English. Orchids, unlike any flowers ever before seen, became a sensation overnight. Here were plants from exotic foreign lands that bloomed without soil and had striking flowers, no doubt because they devoured live insects and even animals! These oddities were so beautiful, so bewildering to the great gardeners of the times that they became an obsession with the English aristocracy. Orchids were treated more like performing animals than like plants and were enclosed in tight glass houses (conservatories) with little or no air. This treatment was administered in good faith, because at the time all the amateur gardener knew about orchids was what the orchid hunters said: that they came from dank, humid jungles.

By 1815, some logic surfaced. Conrad Loddiges, editor of a garden journal and himself an avid gardener, put orchids in well-ventilated areas under glass and watered them frequently. For the first time since their arrival on the scene, the plants thrived. By 1830, orchids were being more sensibly treated, and soon orchidmania set in. The orchid became the fashionable flower of the time. The craze that gripped England had no rival, not even the 17th-century tulipmania that caused such havoc in the Netherlands. By 1840, collectors were sent in droves to all parts of the globe to collect orchids, and the plant auctions at Stevens Rooms, King Street, Covent Garden, and other establishments were fraught with the excitement and fervor of a racetrack. Orchids were sold for incredible sums, as much as $600 for a single large Cattleya.

The importing of orchids reached its peak between 1850 and 1870, but four-fifths of the orchids died in transit; it was often months before the plants arrived in England from their faraway habitats. But because orchids were rare (indeed, most were killed off), the demand soared and there were never enough plants.

During World War I, many fine orchids were destroyed because of lack of fuel to heat the vast greenhouses of companies such as Sander. By 1930, importation of orchids almost ceased. Nurseries were started in tropical countries, and America and Europe made great strides in orchid hybridization, cultivating plants on a very large scale. In America, in the years following World War II, plants were imported from foreign countries. Most survived and were raised successfully by commercial growers. And even before meristem culture (cloning) became common two decades ago, such commercial growers as Hausermann in Villa Park, Illinois (which formerly grew roses), switched to orchids. The flowers were in great demand for corsages, and the budding regiment of orchid hobbyists started to search for sources of plants.

When I started collecting orchids in 1959, I was easily able to buy collected species from several suppliers. But as the jungles were stripped for timber plantations or other developments, and endangered species acts mandated (fortunately), orchids became scarce. Today it is rare indeed that one can obtain jungle-collected plants. But thanks to meristem culture, orchids have again become plentiful and have now emerged as the houseplants of the 1980s.

Today orchids are better than ever. They are beautiful, they have longer-lasting flowers, and many varieties can tolerate cool or warm conditions. There are orchids for almost every possible situation and purpose. The hybridists have taken out all the bad and put in all the good attributes of a living plant. Today, when people see the hundreds of orchids in bloom in my shop, they are amazed at the panorama of color and beauty; it is hard to convince them that they are looking at plants conceived in laboratories. Many people still believe that orchids come from the steaming jungles of the world, and the old Hollywood movies showing fictional and mysterious man-eating plants have not helped the orchids' reputation either.

The orchid is better equipped to withstand the rigors of home culture than ferns, palms, philodendrons, and other green houseplants. Basically, most orchids have pseudobulbs that store water and nutrients in case we forget to water the plants. Despite their delicate appearance and fragile-looking flowers, most orchids have tough foliage that is resistant to insect attack, and the plants are generally very robust, self-sustaining, and hardy, with a strong will to survive imbedded in their genes.

Foliage plants are fine for green ambience in a room, but colorful flowers offer more beauty. And with flowering plants there is also the satisfaction of personally bringing them to bloom, of seeing an orchid grow from a small plant to maturity. And year after year, orchids reward your care with flowers, sometimes twice a year. Many Cattleyas bear flowers semiannually, and some Phalaenopsis blossoms stay fresh on the plants for months!

You can grow orchids as a hobby—there are thousands of orchid hobbyists—or you can raise only a few plants for interiors. There is nothing more graceful than a wand of Phalaenopsis flowers gracing a table or desk, or a striking red Cattleya adding a dramatic touch of color to a living room. When artfully arranged in handsome containers, orchid flowers are arrangements of nature and far outlast any cut flowers. Today roses can cost $40 or more a dozen (£15 or more in Britain), a mature Cattleya orchid with flowers costs about $25 (£15-20 in Britain). Orchids offer a choice of colors that is mind-boggling: contrasting colors, delicate hues, dramatic tones, multicolored extravaganzas. And flower sizes range from small to large. Because of their vast selection and ease of culture, orchids outnumber any other plant for indoor decoration and as a hobby.

It is convenient to grow orchids in a greenhouse, garden room, or atrium because having the plants in one area creates a more lavish and lush setting and makes watering and feeding easier. But a specific place is not a necessity; most orchids will do very well at a window or near some natural light. Certain species of orchids, such as the light-demanding Vandas and some Dendrobiums, require a glass house, but hybridists are now crossing the light-demanding orchids with species that need less light, to create plants that grow in subdued light. For example, Ascocendas are Vandas crossed with Ascocentrums. These plants, with their striking colors, resemble Vandas but need less light than the original Vanda species. Thus almost all orchids have taken their rightful place in the home—finally.

Introduction: The Number One Houseplant

It has been more than twenty years since I wrote *Growing Orchids at Your Windows*, the first book about growing botanical orchids indoors published in the United States. In 1963, orchids were considered only for the wealthy and as greenhouse subjects. Today, orchids decorate rooms in thousands of homes, and there is a legion of hobbyists. Orchids do grow and bloom indoors, and the plants cost no more than the ubiquitous philodendrons or ferns. Thanks to the amazing work of hybridists and the advent of meristem culture, you can now buy an orchid for only $15 or $20 in the United States and Canada, or for £15 or £20 in Great Britain. And perhaps more important, the orchid you buy today is a better plant than its predecessors.

My 1963 book, which is still in print, includes some two hundred species orchids—plants (free from human hands)—and directions on how to grow them. Here I have concentrated on the many new intergeneric hybrids of the past twenty years that have helped make orchids such popular houseplants: Cattleya, Phalaenopsis, Odontoglossum, Oncidium, Paphiopedilum, and other genera. There is little cultural information about growing these complex hybrids; this book, I hope, will fill that void and help you to have blooming plants at home all year.

The cultural information about the plants was gathered during the last several years at my orchid shop, the Garden District in the Napa Valley, California. Here I have grown thousands of different kinds of orchids from Alicearas to Zygopetalums. I grow some plants under glass, others in a garden room, and still others in an average room that serves as a display area.

In addition to advice on growing these orchids, this book contains a generous selection of photographs and line drawings for identification. Here are orchids for every place and everyone, enough flowers and beauty to dazzle the eye and bring solace to the soul for the next twenty years.

Part One:
Knowing And
Growing Orchids

1

The Orchid Family

The orchid family contains the largest number of flowering plants known: more than 35,000 wild species—most of which are becoming very rare these days—and thousands of hybrids. The species orchids grow in the wild, but most hybrids result from human beings having mated the plants bearing the best or the most desirable characteristics with other plants bearing other particularly desirable characteristics. For example, an orchid with large but poorly colored flowers might be mated to a plant with small but brilliantly colored blossoms, such as a Cattleya mated with Sophronitis (brilliant red flowers) to produce a plant bearing large and vividly colored flowers.

Orchid Facts and Fantasy

Although it has been over one hundred years since people began cultivating orchids, certain misconceptions common about the plants still persist. These include the fallacies that orchids are parasites, orchids are difficult to grow, and orchids require greenhouse conditions. The orchid is *not* a parasite; although it uses the branches of trees as a support, it derives no nourishment from the host tree.

Orchids are no more difficult to grow than other houseplants; indeed, many are easier to cultivate indoors because they have pseudobulbs that store water and nutrients. And greenhouse culture, so emphasized in the late 19th century, is vastly overrated—although having a separate place for orchids does mean convenience to the grower. Orchids require a good buoyant atmosphere—air must circulate—but they do not need or want the excessive humidity or scorching sunlight of a greenhouse. Indeed, such conditions will kill orchids.

Orchids are either epiphytic (growing in air) or terrestrial (growing in the ground). Most orchids lead an arboreal life in trees or on rocks. A few, like Cymbidiums and Paphiopedilum, grow in the ground. The orchid plant itself is the most advanced plant we know, has great tenacity, and can endure untoward conditions in cultivation if necessary and still survive. The leaves of many orchids are tough, almost succulent in texture. Cattleyas are a prime example: They can tolerate rough handling if necessary. Orchid foliage is generally immune to insect attack because the leaves are too tough.

In nature, the roots of most orchids are scandent. The aerial roots do not like to be confined; they have to be in the air to absorb any available moisture. We grow orchids in pots merely to anchor the plants. Orchid containers of the early 1900s had holes or slits on the sides so air could circulate freely around the roots.

When they become too large, most orchids can be divided; they can be separated—four growths to a pot—to be grown on. Separation (division) can be as easy as dividing a fern or other clumping plant (see Chapter 4 for a more detailed discussion of propagation).

Orchids can live for decades if properly cared for (and in some instances even if not well cared for). I have several plants that are over twenty years old and have required little care. Generally, such large plants are eventually divided, but I have grown mine on to specimen size.

Botanically, orchids belong to the flowering plants called monocotyledons. They bear a single seed leaf, or cotyledon, on germination; additional leaves are then produced from the center of the stem, passing outward. True bark is absent, and leaves usually have parallel veins. The parts of the flower (petals and so on) are in threes or multiples of three. Dicotyledons, on the other hand, produce two or more seed leaves on germination; young wood forms on the outer part of the stem; leaves are generally netted with veins; and flowers, sepals, petals, and stamens are in fours or fives or multiples of these numbers.

Orchids have made such great advances in flower structure that the family is unique in the plant world. With their intricate structure and ingenious methods of pollination, orchids function at the highest level of efficiency.

Most people believe that orchids come from steamy jungles or rain forests. This is hardly true. Most orchids are treetop dwellers in tropical rain forests at elevations of about 5,000 feet where it is quite cool at night and the plants are always in areas of good air circulation.

While some orchids may grow on the forest floor in constant heat (75°F day and night), for every 1,000 feet the temperature drops about 7°. Since most species grow at 2,000 to 6,000 feet, the temperatures range from 50°F at night to 90°F during the day.

South America—especially Chile, Peru, Ecuador, and Colombia—is rich in orchids, and there the orchids inhabit trees as well as sides of mountains. New Guinea has a vast population of orchids, and Asia,

Africa, Borneo, and Central America also are home for orchids. Hawaii, often called the Orchid State, has no indigenous orchids. (Plants were brought there and are now grown commercially.)

Years ago plants were imported, but not very often today. Most countries no longer allow exportation of native orchids, and others have strict quotas. Although jungle plants are occasionally available, 95% of all orchids sold now are created in laboratories. Hybridists have bred plants of superior 'quality, taking out all the bad features and putting in all the good ones, so today orchids can grow in your home like other houseplants.

Species

The species orchids of years ago—plants from native habitats—are now practically nonexistent. Most countries prohibit exportation of native species, and in many areas where once orchids flourished, the land is now used either for farms or for various types of development. However, the species are still being cultivated, thanks to dedicated orchid growers. The more popular species are being propagated by seed or by meristem culture, for example, *Zygopetalum mackayi*, with its desirable blue flowers. Other beautiful species are also coming into the limelight: *Brassia verrucosa* and *Brs. gireoudiana* are now available from seed or meristem culture, and hybridization is allowing the mating of the best plants in these lesser genera to produce outstanding flowers. Brs. Rex is a prime example.

Size

At one time, Cattleya orchids were basically large, about 22 to 36 inches tall, but hybridization has scaled many of them down to smaller sizes—to accommodate smaller areas in the home. We now have dwarf varieties of Cattleya that are only 14 inches tall. The dwarfs are sometimes called cocktail orchids, art shade orchids, or, occasionally, japhets. There are also miniature Cattleyas such as *Brassolaeliocattleya* 'Wabash,' which grows to 10 inches. These plants are suitable for coffee tables, bookshelves, and other display areas. Note that the term "miniature" also is commonly applied to Cymbidiums (to 20 inches), but "dwarf" is a more descriptive term. (The above miniatures should not be confused with true lilliputian natural species orchids such as *Cattleya citrina* or *C. walkeriana*.)

Thousands of true miniatures grow to only 6 or 8 inches, such as *Laelia pumila* and *Sophronitis grandiflora*. These orchids are discussed in my book *Miniature Orchids to Grow and Show* (New York: Norton, 1981).

Flowers of the Four Seasons

Orchids have been called the flowers of the four seasons because some plants bloom in spring and summer and others in fall and winter. Generally, orchids bloom once a year, but hybrids bear flowers twice or even three times a year, thanks to their mixed parentage. Flowers are produced in a rainbow of colors, with yellow and brown predominating, as in many Oncidium and Odontoglossum hybrids. Apple green appears frequently, but ironically, lavender, the color of the old-fashioned Cattleya, is not very common, nor is true pink. Scarlet, orange, blue, and virtually all other color combinations are found, except true black, which does not exist. The so-called black orchid, *Coelogyne pandurata*, has a very dark green-purple lip. Colors may also be very delicate pastels, or they may be vibrant and bold, as in many hybrid Paphiopedilums.

There is a remarkable range in the size and texture of orchid flowers. Some Bulbophyllums have flowers only $1/32$ inch in diameter, but certain Sobralias flaunt flowers 7 inches across. Some flowers have a texture you can almost see through, while others, such as Ascocentrums, have sepals and petals that look crystalline in sunlight, and many Paphiopedilums have a waxy texture.

Just as the flowers themselves are diversified, so is the method of bearing blooms. Many species have a solitary bloom on a short stem; others have hundreds of flowers on a short stem. Flowers may come from the base of the plant, as in Lycaste, or appear on stems from the leaf axils, as with Angraecums and Vandas. The stems may be pendant, reaching 5 or 6 feet in length in *Dendrobium superbum*, or they may be stiffly erect, to 9 feet high in *Schomburgkia tibicinis*. Some Trichopilias bear flowers that hug the pot rim, and Acinetas and Stanhopeas bear flowers on vertical 3- or 4-foot stems. Many Cirrhopetalums and Bulbophyllums produce flowers in a cluster of thirty or forty blooms that creates a stunning spherical bouquet.

About 80% of orchids are very fragrant. *Lycaste aromatica* has a pleasant cinnamon scent. The odor of musk is easily discerned in *Dendrobium moschatum*. *Maxillaria atropurpura* has a delicious scent of violet. *Dendrobium superbum* smells like rhubarb, and the aroma of *Oncidium ornithorhynchum* is reminiscent of newly mown hay. Many Angraecums and Aerides have a fragrance much like that of gardenias, and *Brassavola nodosa* is so sweetly scented that one flower perfumes an entire room. *Stanhopea mexicana* has a medicinal scent of menthol or camphor, most noticeable in the morning or early evening.

Most orchid flowers stay fresh far longer than roses or carnations do. Cymbidiums are vibrant on the plant for two months; Cattleyas last about a month. When cut and placed in a vase of water, many species of Oncidiums last more than four weeks, and Odontoglossum flowers remain colorful on the plant for six weeks. A few orchid blooms, however, are short-lived: Stanhopeas last only a few days, and Sobralias fade in three days.

Common Names

Common orchid names are often associated with animals or insects (butterfly orchid, moth orchid, bee or spider orchid, foxtail orchid) because the shape of the flower resembles a particular insect or part of an animal. Orchid names may also have religious connotations: *Peristeria elata* is the Holy Ghost orchid; *Lycaste skinneri var. virginalis* is the white nun; and *Epidendrum radicans* is the crucifix orchid; all are so-named because of the shape of their flowers. The Mexican *Schomburgkia superbiens* is known as Saint Joseph's staff, and *Oncidium tigrinum* is the "flower of the dead" because it blooms on All Souls' Day and is used to decorate graves. Perhaps the loveliest name is *Phalaenopsis amabilis*; in Java, this is the moon orchid, so-called because its blooms last longer than a moon, a month or more.

Orchid Hybrids

Recently, when a yellow Cattleya was created to tolerate 40° F or lower outdoor temperatures, it made national news. Hybridization, as we said earlier, is done to create flowers and plants that have more desirable traits: more floriferousness, better flower color, more frequent blooms, ability to grow in a wide range of temperatures, and so on.

People have always tried to improve on nature; perhaps more hybrids have been produced in the orchid family than any other. The process of transferring the pollen from one orchid to the stigma of another to create an orchid with the best characteristics of each parent began about 1869. John Dominy, the grower at the Veitch nursery at Exeter, in England, used *Paphiopedilum barbatum* and *Paph. villosum* for his experiment. He wanted long-lasting flowers on tall stems. The first Paphiopedilum hybrid, called *Paph. harrisianum*, was named in honor of Dr. Jon Harris, a surgeon who first suggested to Dominy the feasibility of mixing plants. The results were successful, and so human beings took over the insects' role in creating new flowers. However, the process was tedious and took time: about seven years from seed to flower.

What happens when certain plants are crossed with other plants? Can the amateur know by looking at a plant what is in it?

Let's use the basic Cattleya as an example. The wild or species Cattleyas (*C. amethystoglossa, C. aclandiae, C. skinneri*) usually have small flowers with a small lip but excellent colors. By adding into the mix some *Brassavola digbyana*—a plant with a massive fringed lip—the hybridists were able to create a Cattleya with a beautiful ruffled lip. Then the breeders decided to insert some Laelia lineage because many species of Laelias have large flowers. Large Cattleya with large lips were produced; these hybrids are called Brassolaeliocattleyas. Then more vivid coloring was wanted (red, for example), so the hybridists looked to the small-flowered wild Sophronitis genus, whose plants have vivid red flowers. Sophronitis were added to the mixture, in time producing the red Cattleyas called Potinaras. Even better reds were produced when it was found that *Laelia milleri*, a small red species, mated well with the Cattleya group.

Within these four genera (Laelia, Brassavola, Cattleya, Sophronitis), most of the Cattleya hybrids have been developed. Recently crosses have been made between Epidendrums and Cattleyas to produce Epicattleyas—somewhat small plants with multiple flower heads. Although the colors are vivid and plants are floriferous, to my mind this has not been a very outstanding cross.

In other genera extensive work has been done with Odontoglossums, Oncidiums, Brassias, Cochliodas, and Miltonias. But not all crosses are outstanding; it is up to the various expert orchid societies to decide which ones are. There have been a great many worthless crosses and a great many worthy ones. You be your own judge. I know from experience that many of the plants I grew that had Miltonia "blood" left much to be desired. Stems were weak, and colors faded in many instances. This is only one personal observation however; no doubt there are many highly desirable hybrids with Miltonia heritage.

When an outstanding cross does result, it is cloned, so that thousands of plants can be made available to the public—each plant an exact replica of the parent. Growers with stellar crosses can demand high prices for their work; thus many growers do hybridizing. A meristem plant such as Maclennara Pagan Lovesong or Vuylstekeara Cambria 'Plush' invariably becomes popular.

The thing to remember is that each genus contributes something to the ultimate marriage. Going back to our Cattleya example, we find the Laelia gives large flowers; the Sophronitis, red color; the *Brassavola digbyana*, the ruffled lip; and so on. The clues to the heritage are in the wild species' *color, form,* and *floriferousness.* In Part Two you will find a description of the various species of each genus.

The breeding of hybrids has satisfied many demands. The cut flower industry has benefited greatly by having superior flowers it can send to market that will last a long time. Growers in warm climates can cultivate cool-growing orchids; those in cool climates can cultivate warm-growing orchids. For example, the marriage of the cool-growing Odontoglossums and the warm-growing Miltonias creates Odontiodas, which tolerate a wider range of temperatures.

Today, a primary reason for hybridization is conservation. Two clones of the same species are bred with each other. Thus the species can be propagated in nurseries, enabling hobbyists to enjoy the many endangered species and, more important, guaranteeing that the plants will be available.

Nomenclature

The nomenclature for hybrid orchids often confuses the would-be hobbyist. For example, what does Blc. Acapana 'Miles' HCC/AOS (Lc. Grande × Greenheart) mean? Blc. stands for *Brassolaeliocattleya*; Acapana is the hybrid name; 'Miles' is a selected clone or varietal name, denoting a single seed-grown individual; HCC means the plant was awarded the Highly Commended Certificate; and AOS denotes an American Orchid Society winner. (AM would denote Award of Merit.) Lc. Grande × Greenheart is the lineage. The Royal Horticultural Society's *Sander's List of Orchid Hybrids* gives you this information. This is the internationally recognized name worldwide; its name and description of flower and color are the same everywhere in the world. It is your assurance of getting the plant you want.

Within each hybrid group are many different clones, each with a clonal name called a *cultivar*. These names are always enclosed in single quotation marks to distinguish one clone (or variety) from others—'Miles,' for example.

Species names are not so complicated because there is no lineage to work from. Basically, *Lycaste aromatica*, for example means the plant comes from the genus *Lycaste*, and the species is *aromatica*. However if you hybridize this plant with other *Lycaste* species, the resulting hybrid might be Lycaste 'Amber Gold.'

Orchid names change as time goes on, and taxonomists rename certain genera based on new findings. For example, many Epidendrums are now called Encyclias, and some Miltonias are now Miltoniopsis. Spellings may vary as well, depending on which books you consult.

Generally I have tried to place plants in their genus as they are accepted by most growers and as they are listed in suppliers' catalogs.

I have used the widely accepted names instead of trying to define the borderline species that still puzzle taxonomists.

All plants mentioned here are usually available, either as mature plants or as seedlings. Several times I have taken the word of a specific grower about the potential of a new variety and included it in these lists.

As a general guide to plant names and spelling I have used the Royal Horticultural Society's *Dictionary of Gardening* (four volumes) published by Clarendon Press, Oxford, 1965.

Cloning

A dramatic change in hydridization occurred in 1961 when Professor George Morel of the University of Paris meristemmed the first orchids. He used the technique developed in 1946 at the University of California for other plants.

Meristem culture (cloning) is a miracle of nature. The technique seems complicated but is basically simple. The apical meristem is separated from the base of a developing young growth within a plant. This tiny shoot is carefully dissected and placed in a liquid medium in a sterile flask. The flask is then placed on a revolving wheel, or agitator; the constant motion inhibits the formation of a growing shoot or root so that the tiny apical meristem multiplies into many protocorms or embryo plants that are then divided. The process can be done repeatedly, thus creating a large number of plants that are exact replicas of the parent. These plants are then replanted and grown on as seedlings. The growth habit and flower color will exactly duplicate those of the mother plant, and the mericlones (the new plants) will flower each year at the same time the mother plant bloomed, which is a vital factor in the cut flower industry. For hobbyists, meristemming has reduced the price of top-quality orchids, making the very best plants available to and affordable for almost everyone. Meristemming is also a boon to conservation because it helps prevent the extinction of certain species.

Meristem culture is exacting and must be done with infinite care and under sterile conditions; it is thus best left to orchid specialists and laboratories. You can send your seed to a lab and have the process performed for a fee. Here, however, is an overview of the basic technique if you want to attempt the process yourself:

1. Cut the pseudobulb from the orchid. Do not remove any compost with it.

2. Carefully and one at a time peel back the leaves that surround the bulb.
3. Expose the shoot by further dissection and immerse the entire bulb in a weak solution of domestic bleach. Rinse off the bleach with deionized water (obtainable from a drug store or chemist).
4. Locate the microscopic meristem area of the growing shoot using a stereoscopic dissecting microscope; then dissect the meristem.
5. Transfer the meristem to a liquid nutrient solution in a flask. Agitate the flask on a wheel or other device so that no shoots or roots can develop. A mass of cells will form.
6. Cut the cell mass into several smaller pieces; these can be grown on to produce more cell masses or to develop into plantlets.
7. To create more cell masses, return the cut pieces to the nutrient solution. If you want seedlings now, place the cut pieces on nutrient agar gel, where they will grow on and eventually become small plants, which you can put into sterile potting mix.

Outstanding Varieties

Within the orchid world certain plants have gained great recognition; like Hollywood stars, they are beautiful and glamorous and sought after. I doubt if flowers can have charisma, but certain varieties do outshine others and become the favorites. For example, Vuylstekeara Cambria 'Plush' is rightly a star. With its beautifully formed flowers in deep maroon contrasted with white, this orchid immediately attracts attention. Couple this with the fact that it is easier to grow than most orchids, and immediately you have a star performer.

Judging from people's reaction to orchid flowers in my shop, the following are the plants that attract the most attention and are the most popular.

Ascocenda Elizabeth Kendall	Very beautiful pink hybrid; flowers spotted and tessellated—a real winner
Brassia 'Rex' (*Brs. verrucosa* × *Brs. gireoudiana*)	A superb cross that produces wands of billowy, creamy white flowers with elongated sepals and petals—always desirable

Brassolaeliocattleya Greenwish 'Elmhurst' AM/AOS	A superb green Cattleya; long-lasting flowers
Cymbidium Cameliard 'Sunshine'	A handsome, clear yellow flower
Odontocidium Tiger Hambühren	Willowy wands with charming yellow and brown flowers; vibrant
Odontoglossum Anneliese Rothenberger 'Floricultura' AM/AOS (*Odm. bictoniense* × *Odm. Goldrausch*)	An incredibly beautiful multi-colored flower; blooms twice a year
Phalaenopsis Paula Hausermann 'Sunshine'	An unbeatable yellow
Phalaenopsis Winter Carnival 'Carousel'	Large white flowers stained red; very handsome
Potinara Rebecca Merkel 'Denise Trowbridge' AM/AOS	A remarkable red
Vanda Hilo Princess 'Alice' AOS/AM	The fantastic blue Vanda; large flowers
Vuylstekeara Cambria 'Plush'	Exquisite red flowers marked with white; a tapestry of color

More popular plants are listed under separate genera headings in Part Two of this book.

2

Buying Orchids

At one time, orchids were offered by a few dealers: mail-order suppliers and an occasional florist shop. Now there are many mail-order suppliers throughout the country, as well as numerous specialty orchid shops, some florist shops, and, as I write this, many outdoor nurseries. So the availability of orchids, limited years ago, is now sufficient.

You should know certain things about orchids so you can get the most for your money when you shop. Should you buy seedlings or mature plants? How do you tell the difference between a healthy specimen and a waning plant? Should you buy orchids out of bloom (cheaper) or in bud? And how much should you pay for specific plants? I'll cover these important factors in the following pages.

Cost

Orchid seedlings are excellent buys: a three-year-old plant in a 4-inch pot that will probably bloom the following year costs about $15 (£7–£10 in Britain). Besides their low price, seedlings offer you another advantage: you can grow the orchid yourself and bring it into bloom. Most seedlings are sold in 3- or 4-inch pots by mail-order suppliers. You can also buy compots (community pots) with twenty or so seedlings to a container; it takes an additional year or two to bring these plants to bloom, but compots cost less than three-year-old seedlings.

The disadvantage of the small plants (ten or twenty to a compot) is that they are more sensitive to new conditions and require more attention and care than, say, plants in 3- or 4-inch pots, which generally flower on the next growth. Plants from compots require several pottings to mature in 4-inch containers.

Many people buy seedlings, but most purchase mature orchids, generally in bloom, in 4-or 5-inch pots. The advantage of buying an orchid in flower is that you see what you are getting: the exact color of the flowers, the size, and so on.

Which is the better purchase? It depends on how much time and care you can give your plants. With either an orchid seedling or a mature plant, look for leaves with substance (firm to the touch), good color (green or shades of green), and fresh *white* root growth.

How much should you pay for an orchid plant? You can buy a perfectly acceptable Cattleya in bloom for about $25 to $30 (about £20 in Britain). You will have a wide choice of color in that price range; flower should be good; and your investment will grow as the plant grows. You can also pay more money for an awarded plant—an American Orchid Society winner, for example—and you can pay an exorbitant amount—up to $100—for a new introduction that has captured the market. (Collectors and many hobbyists seek awarded plants, and many of these people like to be the first on the block to have, say, that rare all-green Cattleya orchid.) Generally the $25 plant is the best buy, however. The award winners will eventually come down in price as more meristems are produced, and the new introductions in time also will become available at more modest figures, as even newer introductions replace them.

Because prices do fluctuate, you should do some comparison shopping. Certain growers are more expensive than others, but most major suppliers of orchids publish catalogs, so you can compare prices. You'll find a wide range of costs, and there are orchids in every price category for everyone.

Recently, there has been a plethora of packaged orchids—some in cellophane bags, others smartly done in plastic bubbles—at low prices. These plants are cheap, but will take more care and time to grow these seedlings into mature blooming plants. Usually the packaged orchids are years away from blooming. If you are aware of this fact and have the time and patience to care for baby plants, this might be a worthwhile purchase.

Many people come back from Hawaii with tiny orchid plants, hoping for a miracle—orchid flowers in their home in a year or so. Again, the chances are slim. Most of the tourist orchids sold in Hawaii are just that—mementos of the trip that may or may not last a few months or longer. As I mentioned before, orchids are not indigenous to Hawaii; they are grown commercially there because of the benevolent climate, but are not native to the islands.

Selection

Indications of a sick or unhealthy plant are limp foliage, no root activity, insect and disease damage on foliage (small pits on leaves, scars, soft areas, general streaking of a color darker than that of the leaves). If possible, select a plant that has fresh new "leads" (sprouts) starting from the previous growth.

Certain orchids, such as some Dendrobiums are deciduous. Inspect the bulbs of deciduous orchids to be sure they are plump and firm, not soft at the base, which could indicate rot.

Most mail-order suppliers sell plants either in pots or bare root. If possible, buy orchids in *plastic* pots—but not in *clay* pots, which weigh a great deal and add to freight costs. Bare root plants are less expensive: about $1 each.

When your plants arrive, pot them immediately; if you cannot do that, at least protect the roots from direct sunlight. Put a newspaper over the plants until you can pot them, but give them sufficient air circulation.

Besides being sold in pots or bare root, orchids are available in spike (bud) or without buds. Orchids in spike or bud cost more than plants that are not in the flowering stage. Generally, it is best to pay the additional $1 or so for plants in bud or spike.

Orchids from Seed or Meristems?

When you buy orchid hybrids grown from seed, you take your chances, because you cannot see the flower when the plant is in the seedling stage. The results of a seed crossing can be, and usually are, variable, and colors of the blooms may differ from those of the parents. Generally, seed-grown plants do turn out as expected, but there is no guarantee when you buy, say, Laeliocattleya Amber Glow 'Marion,' that it will duplicate its parent; there could be variations. The only sure way of getting a true seed-grown plant in the color you want is to buy it in bloom.

When you buy meristems, however, the individual plants will very likely be exact duplicates of the parents. The miracle of cellular division generally guarantees an exact replica of the mother plant, but recently some variation has shown up in this process.

Award Designations

When you are buying orchids, check out varietal names; generally, any orchid that carries an award designation will be a high-quality plant. The awards include AOS (American Orchid Society), FCC (First Class Certificate), and RHS (Royal Horticultural Society). Plants with these designations have been judged for some outstanding characteristic—large flowers, abundance of bloom, color—and have been designated as the best. Expect to pay a little more for an awarded plant than for one without credentials.

The plant lists in Part Two include the awards given to the plants, to help guide your purchases. Are plants without awards a good buy? Certainly. There are thousands of plants that may not be up to the stringent judging of the various societies, but in their own way they are very beautiful and desirable. One person's apple pie may be another's indigestion. Buying plants is a matter of personal taste and need. Most people are not too particular about awarded varieties; others dote on them.

Care of Seedlings

Whether you buy meristems or seed-grown young plants, seedlings require more care getting started than do mature plants (blooming size). An orchid in a 2-inch pot is usually three to four years from blooming; 4-inch pots, one to two years; and 5-inch-pot plants, generally about a year away from blooming. Some genera mature more rapidly than others, and within the Cattleya genus there are now mini-Cattleyas that bloom in 3-inch pots.

The younger the plant the more apt it is to succumb to intolerable conditions. It will need some coddling and more attention than you would give to an adult plant.

Keep seedlings warm at night—60° to 65°F, and provide good humidity—40% to 50%. Grow plants in an area where they are protected from sudden temperature fluctuations. Almost all seedling plants require even moisture; the potting medium (fine-grade fir bark) should never be too wet or too dry. Provide good light for seedlings, but avoid direct sun light; bright diffused light is ideal.

Fertilize small plants with weak solutions of 20-10-10 every other week; watch plants to see how they respond to feeding. Any brown-tipped leaves will indicate too much food, so decrease feeding somewhat if this happens.

After six to nine months in 2-or 3-inch pots (when they are almost three years old), the plants will be ready for 4-inch containers and fresh potting medium. Use a somewhat coarser bark then you used for 2- and 3-inch-pot seedlings. Repot the seedlings carefully and take your time; do not tug them from their old containers and plunge them into new mix and pots. Crumble away old bark with your fingers; inspect the roots for rot; if the roots are brown, trim them off. Keep the medium evenly moist, the humidity at 30% to 40%, and a free, fresh flow of air around plants. Give plants somewhat more light now and increase the light source until they are receiving maximum bright light by the end of the year. Lower temperatures are feasible now—60°F at night is adequate for most genera.

By the end of the fourth year plants should be ready for 5- or 6-inch pots and routine adult plant care as explained in Chapter 4. Some growers speed up the four-year program by furnishing artificial light and thereby bringing plants to bloom in three years, and meristemmed seedlings generally bloom before their fourth year; I have had many in the shop that had a first flowering before they were four years old, so the length of time from seedling to flowering plant does vary, and the above information is in broad general terms.

Sources

There are dozens of orchid mail-order suppliers. Companies such as Hausermann in Illinois and Armacost & Royston in California have been growing orchids for decades. These firms are reputable and strive to deliver the finest orchids to you. I have dealt with almost every orchid supplier and have been disappointed only twice. Most mail-order specialists are dependable and supply catalogs either free or for a nominal fee. You'll find a list of U.S. orchid suppliers at the back of this book.

You can also buy orchids from dealers in other countries, and I have done so, but this involves much paperwork. Today most people will find enough growers in their own country to meet their demands. However, I have included a list of international dealers at the back of the book.

If you live near an orchid nursery or shop, by all means buy your plants there where you can see them and make your own selections. Usually prices of nearby dealers will be somewhat lower than those in the mail-order catalogs. Specialty orchid shops in larger cities carry stock of the highest quality. Although these shops' prices may be slightly higher than those of other dealers, the shop owner usually will replace plants that do not perform well for you, provided you have given them the proper care.

You can also find some orchids, such as Cattleyas and Paphiopedilums, at local florists' shops. Here the selection is likely to be limited, however, and prices are generally quite high. Florists have high overheads and must charge compensatory prices, but they are convenient.

Shipping

Years ago, shipping plants could be hazardous to their health, but today, with improved packing materials and the tremendous advance in nationwide delivery service, you can order plants on Monday and have them delivered two days later almost anywhere. This has been a boon to both mail-order suppliers and hobbyists. Of course, there is still no substitute for a trip to a local nursery where you can choose your plant and see what you are getting. But many people do not live within driving distance of such a place, so mail-order shipping is the most practical choice.

In the United States and Canada, air freight is the fastest way to ship plants. This service is efficient and convenient but hardly inexpensive. Sending ten mature plants from, say, the East Coast to the West Coast can cost as much as $150. Rates are based on weight and space consideration, so call first and get all the details. (British growers tend to use British Rail Redstar Service, which costs about £10 and ensures delivery the same day.)

Standard priority air mail shipping from the post office runs a close second to air freight. Plants arrive within a few days, and rates are not exorbitant. There is, however, a size limitation—no parcel over 108 united inches. United Parcel Service (UPS) also offers a shipping service, but my experience with this particular carrier, even over short distances (within a state), has been disappointing. Plants invariably arrived with broken pots, bark out of pots, and plants crushed. However, some people consider UPS excellent.

Rail and bus transport is inexpensive compared with other carriers, but delivery takes at least five days—many times a week or more. This can be all right, depending on what you are having shipped. Check out all these types of shipping; service varies from region to region, so although priority air mail may be excellent for my purposes, for example, it may not be for yours.

Orchid suppliers pack plants with utmost care, using new wrapping and packing materials. Thus there is little danger of damage to plants unless the carrier mishandles the shipment. Generally plants can be shipped at any time of the year, although in extremely cold or very hot weather it is best not to have plants shipped. (Most suppliers, in fact will not ship in very inclement weather). Read suppliers' catalogs carefully; some charge for packing and shipping but others do not.

A great argument persists about whether to ship plants in or out of pots. The bare root method is less costly, and potting an orchid yourself takes little time. Some growers, however, claim plants are set back by bare-root shipment; others say they are not. I generally order everything shipped out of pot except very large plants, which I find do better when shipped in pots.

3

Orchids Indoors

Years ago orchids were grown in greenhouses. Because they were wild species from the rain forests, people assumed the plants had to be grown in similar conditions. We now know, however, that orchids in cultivation adapt to other environments. About 90% of all orchids can be grown in average home conditions. The orchid has come a long way from the jungle; most plants today, as I've mentioned, are hybrids: the best mated with the best to produce outstanding bloom.

The work done by hybridists to bring orchids into the home has been outstanding. Also, improved home heating and cooling systems make it relatively easy to maintain temperatures at the flick of a thermostat. Indoor lighting and large expanses of glass have brought more light into the home. The queen of flowering plants can thus be grown in almost any room in the house. There is not a nook or cranny in a home that cannot accommodate some orchid.

Orchids today are sold mainly as houseplants. In the 1970s, philodendrons and other green plants were used to decorate the home. Now orchids—much more rewarding in flower and color—are popular. In addition to people who buy orchids as houseplants, there are a large number of orchid enthusiasts—collectors and amateur growers—who cultivate orchids as a hobby. Generally, collectors grow the plants in special areas like garden rooms and atriums. The greenhouse growers, the fanciers of orchids are serious collectors and hobbyists, but they might occasionally sell some plants to interested parties.

Average Home Conditions

Ideal temperatures and humidity are both vital to good orchid growth. Today's home heating and ventilating systems are quite sophisticated; temperatures are controlled by the thermostat, and many houses now have built-in humidity systems. Generally home temperatures range from 55° to 62°F at night and 65° to 75°F during

Plant Pole

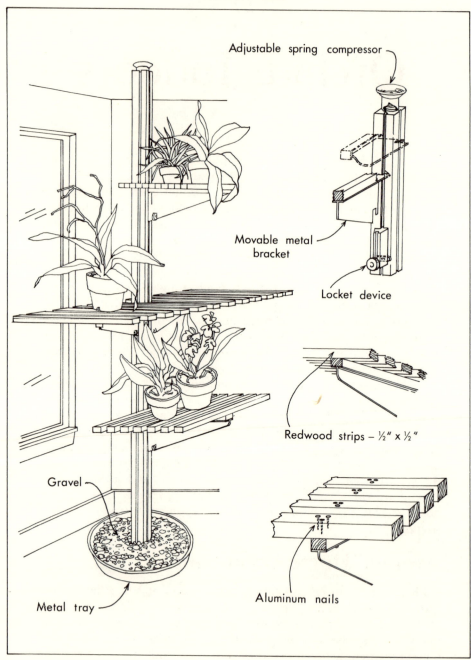

Adjustable spring compressor

Movable metal bracket

Locket device

Redwood strips – ½" x ½"

Gravel

Metal tray

Aluminum nails

Drawing by Carol Carlson

the day, a suitable environment for 90% of the orchids. Humidity may fluctuate from 20% to 50%, depending on outside weather and the time of the year; it may be more humid in summer than winter, for example. Most orchids grow satisfactorily at about 30% humidity, and there are ways of increasing the moisture in the air—using humidifiers for example. Air conditioning, quite common now in homes, helps keep heat down in summer, which is of prime importance because most orchids do not grow well in temperatures over 90°F or in direct sunlight.

Ventilation is perhaps where most homes fall short; a free flow of air is vital for orchids. No orchid will grow in stagnant air. In summer, you can leave your windows open, but in the winter that is impossible in most places. Instead, run a small fan at low speed to keep air circulating. Orchids need a free flow of fresh air, but they do *not* want a draft aimed directly at them—although even that will not kill them.

With the problems of heating, humidity, and ventilation solved, your orchids should flourish indoors as long as you water and feed them. Also, shade your plants from the direct summer sun. Use roll-ups, blinds or curtains to prevent direct, intense sun rays from scorching plants. Remember, your home does not have to be a jungle for you to grow orchids. Indeed, if the conditions are comfortable for you, they will be for your orchids, too.

In rented homes, heat and humidity are sometimes controlled by the landlord. However, most cities have laws that require a certain amount of heat from 7:00 A.M. to 11:00 P.M. Anything under the norm—and this figure fluctuates in each city—can be considered a violation of your lease. When I first started growing orchids in Chicago in a rented apartment, I had a cold-blooded landlord. He simply did not like heat, so many winter mornings the thermometer in my growing area registered only 50°F. Rather than endure arguments with the man, I used several space heaters to warm up very cold areas; this is still a good method.

Where to Put Plants

Orchids are ideal decorative pot plants for the home. What is lovelier than a graceful Phalaenopsis on a coffee table or a small Cattleya at a window? The plants, as I said, have also attracted legions of collectors who grow them in garden rooms or greenhouses and move them into their homes at bloom time.

In the home, decorative plants are difficult to water if they are on a table, windowsill, or shelf. The water always finds its way to the floor or stains polished surfaces. Also, most orchids like bottom ventilation.

I first started using suspension poles with brackets as places for orchids; the trays were handcrafted. The pole-and-bracket units were originally made for use as bookshelves. This photo, taken over twenty years ago, shows the solarium in my Chicago, Illinois, apartment. (Photo by author)

Small and attractive redwood trays are sold commercially; use them under the pots. Or make your own wooden tray, or use plastic grids (light fixture panels) or any other tray that lets air underneath the plant.

In the home, orchids grow best near a window; a south or east exposure is ideal. At a west window, heat can build up in summer, and direct sun scorches leaves; if you have orchids in a west window, provide the protection I mentioned earlier—even a light curtain helps. In a north window, orchids such as Paphiopedilums and some Odontoglossums will be right at home.

Most orchids—including Cattleyas, Dendrobiums, Laelias, and Brassias—need some diffused sunlight. Many plants, such as

Places for Orchids

Plant shelf and 6" galvanized pan filled with a layer of gravel

Redwood-strip tray above galvanized humidity pan

Fluorescent light fixture over table

Redwood-strip tray directly on galvanized pan

Drawing by Carol Carlson

I built this sun room–garden room some years ago when I moved to California. Orchids predominate. (Photo by Joyce R. Wilson)

Paphiopedilums and Phalaenopsis, are fine in filtered or diffused light but not in direct sun. Your home has dozens of places for orchids; it is merely a question of selecting the proper plant for your light situation.

A friend of mine in Chicago grew her plants on wood slats placed over pie plates on a movable tea cart. In winter she kept the plants in her bedroom at a south window; in summer she moved the cart to an east window in her recreation room. She followed the sun, and her orchids benefited from this decision.

Window Growing and Window Greenhouses

People who are fortunate enough to have windowsills can grow plants on them (windowsills are rarely installed in new construction). A table or plant stand is another fine place for orchids. Search local garage sales for used tables or plant pedestals that will put your plants at the proper height so they can enjoy the most light.

You can also use galvanized metal planters. Fill them with gravel and some water; moisture evaporating on the gravel creates humidity for the plants. Unfortunately, these plant bins are difficult to find and if you have them custom-made (to fit a sill, for example), they are

I built this window greenhouse on the north side of my home; here Paphiopedilums and Cattleyas thrive. Commercial window greenhouses are also available. (Photo by author)

expensive. I was lucky to find some used trays that had held water for radiators, and these work fine. Plastic trays are available, but unattractive. The clear acrylic ones are the least objectionable; each tray will hold four or five plants. Set the trays on a table in front of a window or on a windowsill to create a handsome window picture. Just how you place orchids at windows depends on your ingenuity. I am always on

An airy atrium boasts orchids as decorative accents, and the total effect is beautiful. In such a situation plants provide their own humidity; leaves transpire, furnishing moisture in the air.

the lookout for small tables, trays, used desks, and so forth that are the appropriate size and height for plants. No doubt you will have other ideas; the main one is to place the plant where it will get the most light from the window.

Glass shelves at the window are another possibility. Have the glass cut to size at a local glass house and then nail small strips of molding to the window jamb to accommodate the shelves. A plant-shelf kit is still another idea. Garden magazines advertise these kits; you get three or four glass shelves with suitable hardware for attaching them to the window.

In the past few years, hanging plants have become very popular, and many of the pendant orchids adapt to basket growing. Look for hanging containers that have attached saucers to catch excess water; with other containers you must devise a drip tray on the floor.

Growing orchids at your windows restricts you to plants of a certain height; any orchid taller than 40 inches is cumbersome and unwieldy at a window. Fortunately, today most orchids are smaller versions of their standard cousins. Art shade Cattleyas, for instance, generally grow no taller than 20 inches.

The window greenhouse has become very popular for plants. Kits are sold at lumberyards, home improvement centers, and even some supermarkets. They are generally easy to install. You can also make your own window greenhouse, as I did some years ago, from redwood, acrylic, and glass shelves. My east window addition accommodates about forty plants. In most window greenhouses, there is a height restriction of about 30 inches between shelves. You can always remove a shelf to make more head room, but this will reduce the number of plants you can grow.

Artificial Light

Fluorescent lights have opened new avenues for orchid hobbyists. Today, all kinds of plants flourish under indoor lighting, even in closets, attics, and almost any usable space. Of the new fluorescent lamps for growing plants, Gro Lux is perhaps the most popular. These lamps come in an assortment of sizes and wattages; the basic commercial arrangement employs two or four lamps with suitable trays underneath. You can also make your own light units.

I never successfully grew orchids under fluorescent light. In Chicago, for two dreary winters I repeatedly tried this type of gardening, but with little reward. However, friends of mine do well with orchids

Some orchids grow well under artificial light. Here small Epidendrums grow on a top shelf.

under fluorescent light. They have been at it for years, so I think practice and experiments are the keys to successful fluorescent-light gardening.

Instead of fluorescent lamps, you can use the standard grow bulb that looks like an incandescent lamp but is made specifically for plants. Such reflector fixtures look good and are inexpensive. These lamps are also easy to use. You merely screw them into a socket; no elaborate equipment is needed. In the same vein, floodlamps will furnish some needed light on very gray days. In both cases, aim the lamps at the plant. Keep the bulbs 3 feet from plants, and leave them on twelve hours a day. The cost of energy for a few lamps is not exorbitant, even with today's rates.

Greenhouses and Garden Rooms

In the past ten years, greenhouses have become popular in homes. Most of the greenhouse manufacturers I checked with say that their

My current plant room was built specifically for orchids and faces southeast. The ceiling has two large skylights, and orchids flourish in this environment. (Photo by author)

This photo shows the details of the window construction in my plant room. Note the redwood slats used as trays for orchids and the ceiling construction: partially wood and two skylights. (Photo by author)

business is up 40% to 60%. Made of plastic or glass, greenhouses are available in many sizes and designs. You'll find many types advertised in the garden magazines. Just what you choose will depend on your own tastes and budget. For growing orchids, an adequate greenhouse should be about 16 by 25 feet. This is enough room for many plants (but not too many) and provides a suitably large working area.

Cultivating orchids under glass or plastic is somewhat different from doing so in your home. In a greenhouse the plants will get more light, which greatly encourages growth, but you must increase the watering, watch humidity more carefully, and provide perfect ventilation. If you can't do these things, you would be better off growing plants in a window. Too much humidity and not enough ventilation can lead to many orchid maladies.

You do *not* need separate warm or cool areas in the greenhouse for growing orchids. This procedure began in England in the 1880s but is now considered archaic. Most greenhouses have both warm and cool microclimates; place your plants accordingly. For example, Cattleyas and Laelias need the warmer places; most Miltonias and Odontoglossums need the cooler areas. If by chance a cool-growing orchid gets placed in a warm section, do not worry—eventually the cool orchid will adjust.

An adequate heating system is vital in a greenhouse, but I cannot recommend one type over another. Your greenhouse and your cli-

Cattleya and Phalaenopsis orchids are at home in this atrium with ferns and philodendrons; the total effect is warm and inviting.

mate will determine your needs. Obviously, in Chicago you need a more elaborate heating system than, say, in northern California, where I live.

Ventilation and lighting in the greenhouse need careful consideration. Greenhouses become very hot in summer, and too much sunlight can be detrimental to orchids. Greenhouses should have doors, but some attached units have none. You get additional air circulation through vents, which most greenhouses have. However, be sure your unit has *several* vents to allow air into the area. Install an automatic push-button system. Put the vents on automatic timers so they will open when the temperature goes above 78°F and close when the temperature drops below 60°F. The automatic system is also a great help when you are away from home for a few days.

In a greenhouse, there will be too much hot, direct, intense sunlight for most orchids. With the exception of Vandas and other vandaceous

This custom-built garden room is perfect for orchids; there is ample top light but not too much, doors on all sides for adequate air circulation, and a concrete floor. This area is unheated in winter and temperatures may drop to 45°F. The garden room is in northern California. (Photo by author)

A commercial aluminum and glass greenhouse in Chicago, Illinois, houses many orchids. This greenhouse has automatic temperature control. (Photo by author)

types, orchids like *diffused* light. You must use some type of shading. The old-fashioned method of whitewashing the plastic or glass windows of a greenhouse is time-consuming, but it works. In the shop, I use shade cloth—a green plastic cloth—strung under the glass and over the plants. The cloth can be moved by hand to protect plants on sunny days and to allow light in on days when the sun is weak. This system works fine. The green cloth is sold at nurseries and comes in various size meshes. I prefer the cloth that lets in 30% or 40% of the light. (Check with your nurseryman.)

Adjustable overhead blinds are handsome but very expensive. Most greenhouse manufacturers sell blinds as well as inexpensive bamboo roll-ups that help thwart direct sun.

Watering in a greenhouse does not have to be complicated. Watering each pot separately with a hose is time-consuming, but it's a good way to closely observe each plant. This method has worked successfully for me for years. I can tell at a glance which varieties need water and which do not, and the human hand is quite accurate for controlling a stream of water, so that young, vulnerable growths do not rot from too much moisture.

I water in the morning, two or three times a week. I always water early so that plants will be dry by evening; this eliminates any risk of fungus and mildew. Some growers, however, water at midday, when the light is brightest. I use water direct from the tap, figuring that if I can drink the water, so can the plants. I sparsely water newly potted plants until their roots can accept moisture.

Elaborate spray or misting systems, often recommended in books about greenhouse gardening, are more for the gadget-loving owners than for the orchids. In a greenhouse, because many plants grow together, there will be sufficient humidity, so excessive misting and spraying are not generally necessary. Overhead watering with a hose or misting system may cause moisture to accumulate between leaves, and this can lead to rot. Also, keep in mind that any automatic watering system, including the type used for lawns, will water all plants rather than only those that need it. Since many orchids rest at some time of the year, this can cause havoc.

The garden room has become the newest addition to many homes, an effort to bring the outdoors indoors. This glass-enclosed area—perhaps with some skylights—is a perfect place to grow orchids.

A handcrafted small orchid greenhouse in a yard in Marin County, California. Although quite shaded, orchids do well in this environment. (Photo by author)

There is enough light for plants to flourish but not so much sun that they burn. The usual garden room is today's counterpart to the Victorian solarium and as such provides a pleasant retreat from the stress and strain of everyday life. Here amid greenery and lovely flowers one can forget the cares of the day and relax and refresh oneself.

I have built garden rooms on most of the homes I have lived in—some quite large and a few, small. However, in all cases this addition was worth its weight in gold. It is a superior room for plants and people.

In a garden room, some of the same conditions prevail as in a greenhouse, but with these exceptions: the garden room does not get as warm in summer, and there is no need to shade the plants from direct summer sun. Roof 40% of the room with glass; orchids will thrive in such a situation.

Lean-to commercial greenhouses are popular, and they make fine places for many orchids. Note the roll-up blinds on the glass roof to protect plants from direct summer sun. (Photo courtesy Lord and Burnham)

4

ABCs of Growing Orchids

Humidity and temperature are not great problems in the home for people or plants if certain conditions are met and procedures followed. Growing orchids indoors requires proper watering and feeding, using the right potting mixes, protecting plants from insects or disease, repotting plants at the correct times, and promoting bloom. These requirements are not difficult to fulfill. With time, you will know when to water an orchid by simply looking at it. (You'll know when most plants need water by their limp leaves). And with feeding, vital for proper orchid growth, it is *when to* feed plants, not what brand of food to feed them, that matters most.

Watering

If you can drink the water from your tap, it is safe for your orchids, too. If you live in an area with a high concentration of chloride and fluoride in the drinking water, let the plant water stand overnight so these chemicals can dissipate.

Cold water will not really harm most plants, but tepid water is better. Water in the morning so plants will dry out by nightfall; damp plants in the evening are vulnerable to fungus disease. However, an occasional watering in the afternoon, if necessary, will not kill orchids, which are quite durable. When you apply the water, be sure to moisten all the fir bark (the potting medium); this sometimes requires a great deal of water—if the plant is newly potted, for example. Water at the sink, or in place if you have large saucers underneath the pots. Let the water flow through the pot to the saucer, empty the saucer, and repeat the process. This should thoroughly moisten the potting medium.

Small orchids dry out faster than those in large containers, and

Cattleya Orchid Plant

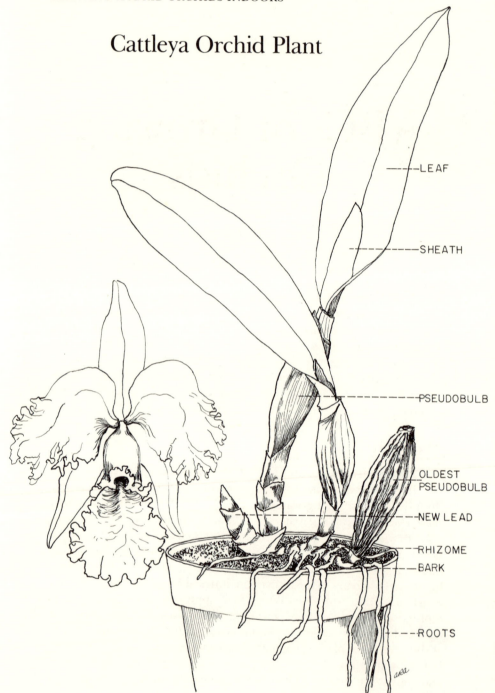

LEAF

SHEATH

PSEUDOBULB

OLDEST PSEUDOBULB

NEW LEAD

RHIZOME

BARK

ROOTS

Drawing by Andrew Addkison

plastic pots retain moisture longer than clay (terra-cotta) pots. However, clay pots release moisture slowly through evaporation, which I believe is good for orchids. Orchids on bark or tree fern slabs dry out very fast and need water more often than plants in pots.

Here is my watering schedule for Cattleyas, Paphiopedilums, Phalaenopsis, Ascocendas, Vandas, Epidendrums, Oncidiums, Odontoglossums, and evergreen Dendrobiums:

- *Plants in 2- to 4-inch clay pots:* four times a week in warm weather; two or three times a week in cold weather
- *Plants in 4- to 7-inch clay pots:* three times a week in warm weather; twice a week in cold weather
- *Plants in clay pots over 7 inches:* Twice a week all year except in winter, then once a week

For deciduous orchids like some Dendrobiums, I follow this watering schedule for all plants in any size container: dry out severely after they bloom; do not water until you see new growth starting. Then water three times a week in spring and summer and once or twice a week in fall and winter. To promote bloom, taper off water and feeding before seasonal bloom time.

Misting and Humidity

Misting foliage can destroy some orchids. Water lodges in young growth and causes rot; water sprayed directly on buds can cause them to drop. The rain forest atmosphere so widely advocated in Victorian times for orchids simply does not work. Once orchids are in cultivation, adequate moisture in the air—say, 30%—is all that is required. If your house is very dry and you must mist plants, spray only the pot and potting medium to provide some temporary humidity.

There are several ways of providing additional humidity for plants at home; perhaps one of the easiest is to set pots on trays of gravel. Use about an inch of gravel and keep the tray filled with water to the top of the gravel. Evaporation will provide some additional humidity. You can also spray the area where plants are grown with a fine mist every day or so in warm weather; this adds some moisture to the air but not a great deal. Of course if you grow many plants, humidity should remain at a safe level without any help from you, because plants transpire through their leaves and a group of plants furnishes its own humidity.

If your house is excessively dry, you might think about purchasing a small room humidifier—the kind that creates a fine, cool mist in the air, not the type used for flu or colds. Or if you have drains and a tile

Types of Flowers

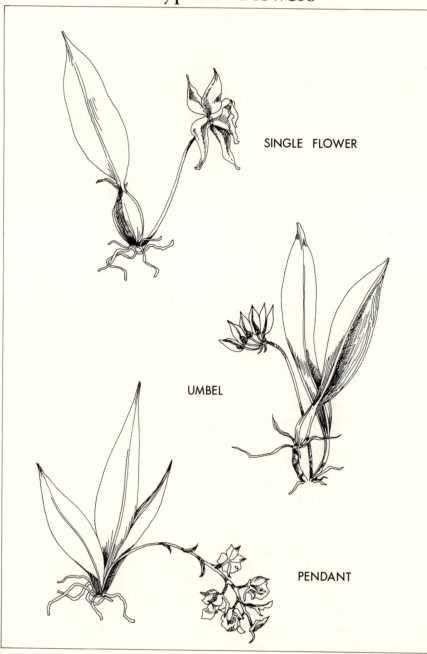

SINGLE FLOWER

UMBEL

PENDANT

Drawing by Carol Carlson

or brick floor, you can simply hose down the growing area on very hot days to furnish humidity for plants.

Feeding

There are many brands of plant foods—Spoon-it, Schultz, Peters, Oxygen Plus (Orchid Quick in Britain)—as well as various types: granules, liquids, systemics with food. Plant foods consist of nitrogen, phosphorus, and potash, marked in that order by percentage on the packages. For example, 30-20-10 means 30% nitrogen, 20% phosphorous, and 10% potash, with the remaining 40% consisting of filler (other elements, mostly). Nitrogen promotes good leaf growth; phosphorous helps stems and flowers; and potash induces general vigor. My experience has been with Peters orchid foods. These foods are made especially for orchids, and in the shop we have had the best results using the various Peters orchid fertilizers. I use the basic 30-10-10 plant food for all-purpose feeding three times a month in warm weather, twice a month in winter. I also use Peters Blossom Booster (10-30-20) during seasonal bloom times, which is in late spring for most orchids, summer for Cattleyas. The food comes in the form of granules, which you mix with water. In each pot, I apply just enough of the solution to moisten the bark. In addition, twice a year I use a mild solution of Atlas Fish Emulsion. I have used this product for decades and find it very satisfactory.

The new time-released fertilizers work well for other houseplants, but I have lost several orchids with them. And, just as I do not believe in overhead watering of plants, I do not believe in foliar feeding—spraying food on foliage—because there is always the possibility of water accumulating in young growths.

Do not apply any plant food when the fir bark is totally dry. Do not apply food when the sun is shining directly on plants, and never feed a sick orchid. Use plant foods on healthy orchids that have been watered and are in a light but not sunny place. Whenever in doubt about any feeding, remember it is better to feed lightly rather than heavily and to feed more when plants are growing than when they are resting.

In areas with cold winter weather, such as the American Midwest or northern Scotland, in January and February stop feeding plants with any solution. In warmer places, a year-round feeding program is beneficial for most orchids. Here is my feeding program for Cattleyas, Paphiopedilums, Phalaenopsis, Ascocendas, Vandas, Epidendrums, Oncidiums, Odontoglossums, and evergreen Dendrobiums:

- *Plants in 4- to 7-inch clay pots:* standard plant food (30-10-10) twice a month from August to January; bloom booster (10-30-20) from February to August
- *Plants in clay pots over 7 inches:* standard plant food (30-10-10) once a month from August to January; bloom booster (10-30-20) from February to August.

This feeding program is based on plants grown in warm areas such as California and Florida. Temper the feeding schedule, as mentioned earlier, for other areas.

It is best to feed plants shortly after they have been watered. Feed regularly and routinely—do not skip a week. If orchids are getting too much food, they will let you know by displaying leaves with brown-tipped edges, burned from too much food. And finally, never try to force a plant to grow; too much food can kill it.

Potting Mixes and Repotting

The following directions apply generally to most types of orchids. Be sure to read the instructions in chapters about specific genera before doing any repotting.

Before the advent of steam-dried fir bark, osmunda was the generally accepted potting medium for orchids. Potting in osmunda was a chore because the material had to be cut and soaked and was difficult to work with. Fir bark is so simple to use that a child can pot an orchid. Bark comes in fine, medium and coarse grades. Medium-grade fir bark generally comes in 1/4-inch pieces (chipped bark). It is sterile, and although it offers orchids virtually no nutrients, it is clean, easy to work with, and relatively inexpensive; a hobby bag that will pot five or six plants costs about $3.00.

I pot my Cymbidiums and Paphiopedilums in fine-grade mix. I grow my Vandas and some Ascocendas in large-grade bark, though, because these plants need air in their root networks and the larger-grade bark provides more air spaces. I grow all my other orchids in medium-grade bark. Some growers in Hawaii and Florida use chunks of charcoal (available in packages at nurseries); others use pieces of pot (shards), and I know some growers who use gravel as a potting medium for orchids. For the average orchid hobbyist, however, fir bark is the usual choice; in Great Britain, pine bark.

When you buy fir bark for your orchids, be sure the package *specifically* states that the material is for orchids. Fir bark is also available as a covering for walks and paths, and this material is different from orchid bark; the pieces are large, and there are many

Mounting Orchids on Bark

Moisten osmunda.

Tie in place with string.

Position plant.

Add osmunda, tie again and mist.

Drawing by Carol Carlson

splinters and much dust in walkway fir bark. The average life of fir bark is about eighteen to twenty-four months; after that time it decays and becomes pulverized. It can become sour and stagnant and thwart root growth.

Most orchids have to be repotted annually or every two years. Here are general rules for repotting. Tap the pot rim lightly on the edge of a table or countertop to loosen the root ball. Then grasp the crown of the plant with one hand, holding the pot with the other hand. Gently tease the plant from the container. Even potting experts occasionally tear a few roots, so do not panic if you break some off.

Once the orchid is out of the pot, gingerly tease away clinging old bark and examine the plant's roots. You can cut off those that are brown or brownish black, but white roots indicate live tissue, so do *not* cut them. Curl the white roots around the base of the plant. In a clean pot (the same size or slightly larger than the used one) place shards and a layer of fresh bark. Put the plant into the pot and fill the pot with bark. Press down the bark occasionally with your thumbs so the plant is securely potted. It should stand upright in the container, not lean one way or another. Loose potting should be avoided.

The rule of thumb is to use a new pot one inch larger in diameter than the old pot, but this is not mandatory; sometimes a plant will fit into a pot of the same size. Generally, I find that orchids grown somewhat potbound (in pots that are slightly too small), especially Miltonias and Dendrobiums, bloom better than those in very large containers.

After repotting, usually it is best not to water immediately. (As there are exceptions, refer to instructions in chapters about specific genera.) Let the orchid rest from the shock for, say, a day or so; put the plant in a shady place for its convalescence. Then start watering. Before repotting, some growers first soak the new clay pot in water a few hours so it will soak up the moisture, but I have found that plants do not really benefit from this practice.

Containers

Unless you are growing miniature orchids or certain species of Laelias, which are generally grown on mounts (slabs of tree fern), your plants will be in containers. I have used standard clay pots for years. Plants grow well in clay because the moisture from the porous walls of the container slowly evaporates, and I like the appearance of terra-cotta pots. However, orchids can also thrive in plastic pots. Because plastic is nonporous, potting mix in a plastic container remains moist longer than a mix in a clay pot. This can be an

Potting with Fir Bark

Place shards in pot.

Add bark.

Tamp down bark.

Tie, stake, and label.

Drawing by Carol Carlson

advantage or a disadvantage. If you live in a warm climate, you can eliminate additional watering if the mix stays moister longer. But in severe-winter climates, excessive retention of moisture in potting mixes can cause fungus to begin forming. Also, plants in plastic pots, which are lightweight, can be top-heavy, unless you put enough ballast (shards, gravel) in the bottom of the pot to balance it. Suspending plastic pots on hangers from the ceiling can be a problem. Usually the rim of a plastic pot will not accommodate the standard wire hanger. This is a detail worth considering, because many orchids like to be suspended close to windows, to get maximum light. Whether plastic or clay, your pots must be scrupulously clean. If you reuse containers, scrub them thoroughly with scalding water and rinse well.

Many kinds of decorative containers are available—jardinieres, cachepots, and urns, for instance—but do not pot directly in these housings. Instead, pot your orchid in clay, and place that pot on a saucer inside the decorative container. The saucer will catch excess water. For a final decorative touch, add green moss (sold in hobby bags) to the top of the pot; this makes the container and plant look handsome indeed. Occasionally replace the moss when you water; after some time, moss becomes water-soaked, and insects might appear.

Plant Protection

If you are growing orchids indoors, you should have little problem with insects because most orchids' leaves are so tough that insects will look elsewhere for more tender fare. And because orchids are not grown in soil, the chances of insect attacks are slim. In soil, insects and insect eggs can hide, but in bark they cannot: you can see them.

Any insects that may attack your orchids will probably be pests from your other houseplants. It is hard to see mealybugs and aphids on philodendrons, palms, ferns, and such because the bugs hide in leaf axils and under leaves. However, on orchids, any insects are usually immediately visible because of the plants' growth structure.

Mealybugs are cottony pests about $\frac{1}{8}$ inch in diameter; aphids are oval-shaped bugs. Scale are brown or blackish oval-shaped insects. To kill these insects, dip a cotton swab in rubbing alcohol and directly touch the pests with the swab. Repeated applications are necessary. If the infestation is severe, consider using a pesticide, such as Malathion-50. I strongly do not recommend this for indoor use, but the choice is yours.

Basically, ants are the most bothersome insects with orchids. They love to hide in the bark and build nests; if ants infest a plant,

Common Insects

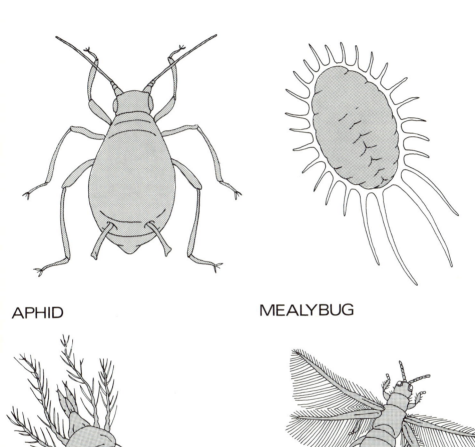

APHID

MEALYBUG

SPIDER MITE

THRIP

Drawing by Bob Johnson

mealybugs are bound to appear, because ants are great herders of mealybugs, establishing colonies of them to provide protein for their young. If you see ants, immediately flush the potting medium with water and then use a good ant repellent. There are several on the market; I have been successful with Grants Ant Stakes.

Slugs and snails adore all plants and will feast on orchids if nothing else is available. A routine dousing with slug and snail bait keeps them away from plants. Corys is an excellent snail and slug bait and also controls ants.

Red spider occasionally attack orchids. This pest cannot be readily seen, but its work can be spotted immediately: silvery leaves and/or streaked leaves. If this happens, you must use a miticide such as Sevin. Keep all insecticides in a high cupboard away from children and pets and use them according to the directions on the package.

Fungus disease (botrytis) can attack orchids if light is not sufficient and if there is too much moisture in the air in the growing area. These infections cause mildewed, powdery, mushy growth. The best preventative is to cut away the infected parts immediately and dispose of them. There are also many chemical fungicides on the market.

Virus disease in orchids is less a problem now than it was, say, a few years ago because most stock used for propagation today is virus-resistant. If you do see streaked or spotted areas (concentric rings) on leaves, remove those leaves immediately and burn them. There is still no dependable chemical preventative for virus in orchids.

With leaf spot, brown spots appear on leaves, usually caused by too-moist conditions coupled with gray days. Carefully cut away the infected leaf and then dust the wound with ground-up charcoal. Keep the plant somewhat dry for the next few days. A good chemical preventative is Benomyl.

Brown spot manifests itself as large and somewhat watery spots on foliage. Splashing water carrying bacteria onto leaves usually causes this malady. Cut away infected parts; dust with charcoal or Benlate paste.

Rust appears as orange or brown raised spots, usually on the undersides of leaves. Cut away infected parts and dust with charcoal. One means of chemical control is to spray with Captan.

Anthracnose is a common disease that causes brown rings and sunken spotting of foliage. Benomyl spray is the only answer.

Grooming

Plants that are well groomed are likely to be healthy. Grooming consists of keeping foliage clean; removing infected foliage; removing

Offset Division

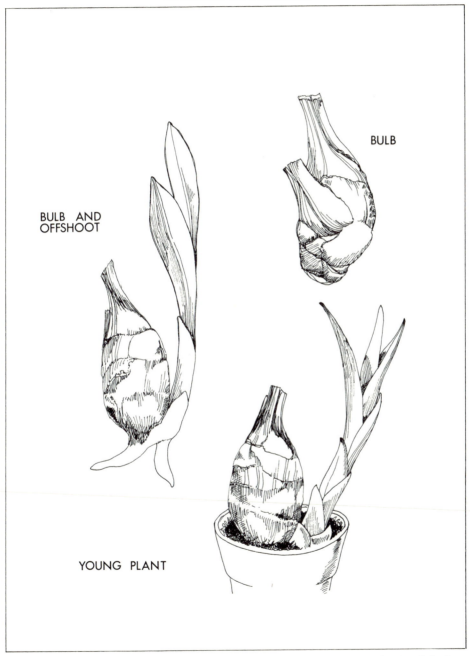

BULB

BULB AND
OFFSHOOT

YOUNG PLANT

Drawing by Carol Carlson

faded flowers and trailing stems immediately; and making sure plants are growing upright rather than leaning. Occasionally wash leaves with a damp cloth; do not use leaf-shining preparations; they can clog pores. A little laundry bar soap on a cloth does the job nicely; flush away the soap with a water spray.

Remove and discard all old flowers before they fall off. Decayed flowers are invitations for fungus disease. With Phalaenopsis, cut the stem above another node to encourage a second flowering. Cut Cattleyas just above the pseudobulb, removing the dead sheath and flower spike. Cut Cymbidiums as close as possible to the bulb.

It is very beneficial to stake and tie Cattleyas and other bulbous orchids. You can use the ring hoops made for this purpose, or devise your own staking.

Propagation

Hobbyists use several methods for increasing their orchid collections: divisions, offsets, backbulb growth, and flower-stem plantlets. Growing orchids from seed is a time-consuming process—you do not see results for seven years or so—and meristemming is best left to experts. Vegetative propagation methods are the answer. These methods are not beyond the ability of even the beginning hobbyist.

Division means dividing a large plant of seven or eight growths (bulbs). You cut off each division (bulb) and pot it. Make the cut with a sharp, sterile knife, although sometimes a gentle twist will divide the plant. Cattleyas, bulbous Epidendrums, Miltonias, Pleurothallis, Odontoglossums, and Oncidiums can all be divided. Spring and summer are the best times to divide plants, because orchids are actively growing then and the warm weather encourages the new plants.

After you divide a plant, put the divisions in a humid and bright location at about 70°F. Do not water for the first few days; let the plant recover from the shock of the surgery. Instead, gently mist the surface of the potting medium a few times a day. After a few days, start routine waterings.

Orchids such as Angraecum and Phalaenopsis frequently form offsets at their base. When the offsets (kikis) have a few roots, twist them free of the mother plant or cut them off. Dip the offsets in Rootone and put them in a separate pot. After a few days, start watering the offsets.

There is an old saying that one should never throw away an orchid backbulb—pot it instead. This is good advice; quite often the backbulbs give rise to a new plant. This method is not always successful,

Division

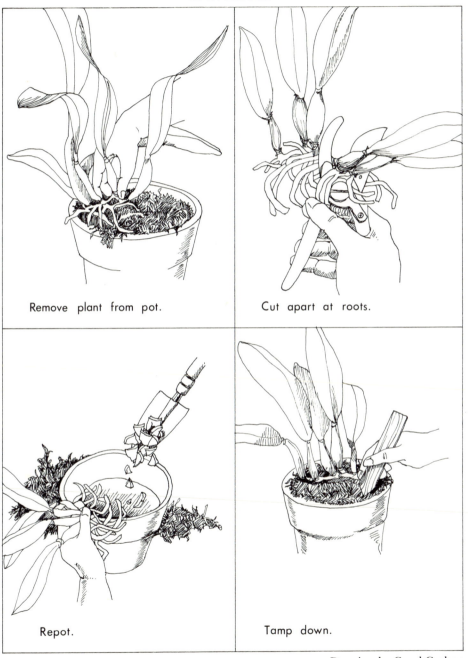

Remove plant from pot.

Cut apart at roots.

Repot.

Tamp down.

Drawing by Carol Carlson

but it does work most of the time. Place the backbulb(s) in trays of vermiculite on plastic bags. Apply water cautiously at first and then give routine humidity and warmth (78°F).

Dendrobiums and Phalaenopsis often produce stem plantlets on their inflorescence. After a few roots form, remove the stem offsets and treat them as you would regular offsets.

Promoting Bloom

People often ask me how they can get an orchid to bloom. My answer depends on the type of plant. I suppose there are some surefire ways of getting plants to bloom, but I don't know them. I do know a few tricks that sometimes will coax an orchid into flower, but usually if plants are well cared for, watered, fed, and given sufficient light, they do bloom naturally in their seasonal time. Nonetheless, here are a few tricks I sometimes use for stubborn performers.

- Dendrobiums: I dry out these plants severely if they have not bloomed on schedule. This works (sometimes).
- Cattleyas: I move them to the uppermost part of the garden room where it is warm and where there is bright light.
- Oncidiums, Epidendrums: I move them about until I find a location they like; sometimes a few inches one way or another makes the difference.
- Phalaenopsis: I decrease evening temperatures to, say, 56°F.
- I do *not* increase feeding for any orchid if the plant does not bloom; too much feeding can harm many orchids.

Cattleyas

Lc. Yung Hua 'Red Top' (Beall Orchids)

Pot. Harlequin Peak 'Orange Princess' (Beall Orchids)

C. Chocolate Drop × *Broughtonia sanguinea* 'Yellow Eyes' (Orchid World Int.)

Blc. Beacon Mt. 'Gaiety' AM/AOS (Beall Orchids)

Pot. Chimney Rock 'The Prize' (Beall Orchids)

Slc. Wendy's Valentine 'June' (Orchid World Int.)

Blc. Oconto 'Yellow Pride' (Hausermann)

Pot. Rebecca Merkel 'Denise Trowbridge' AM/AOS (Hausermann)

Blc. Melinda Wheeler 'Halcyon' HCC/AOS (Hausermann)

Cattleyas

Lc. Hausermann's Sultan 'Summer Spectacular' (Hausermann)

Blc. Mount Triumph 'Wingtip' AM/AOS (Beall Orchids)

Blc. Don De Michaels 'Razzamatazz' (Hausermann)

Blc. Greenwich (Hausermann)

Slc. Vallazac 'Billy Miles' AM/AOS (Hausermann)

Lc. Aqui Finn 'Splish Splash' (Hausermann)

C. Bob Betts 'Mont Millas' (Beall Orchids)

Lc. Mount Juncal (Orchid World)

Bwna. Nora (Orchid World)

Phalaenopsis and Doritaenopsis

Phal. Sun Prairie 'Yellow Star' (Hausermann)

Phal. Paula Hausermann 'Sunshine' HCC/AOS (Hausermann)

Phal. Painted Cave 'York' HCC/AOS (Hausermann)

Phal. Class President 'Willowbrook' (Hausermann)

Phal. Carnival 'Bonsall' AM/AOS (Hausermann)

Hausermannara Lucie Hausermann 'York' (Hausermann)

Phal. Fireball (Hausermann)

Dtps. Pretty Nice 'York' AM/AOS (Hausermann)

Dtps. Ravenswood (Oak Hill Gardens)

Multigeneric Crosses

Odm. Sunshine (Beall Orchids)

Mtssa. Olmec 'Tiger Lilly' (Beall Orchids)

Wils. Five Oaks 'Golden Leaf' AM/AOS (Beall Orchids)

Bak. 'Sambo' (Beall Orchids)

Bllra. 'Lavender Leopard' (Beall Orchids)

Oda. Chignik (Beall Orchids)

Bak. 'Rampart' (Beall Orchids)

Odm. Golden Ransom 'Pride of Vashon' (Beall Orchids)

Oda. 'Jelly Roll' (Beall Orchids)

Vanda and Ascocenda

V. Onomea (Orchid World Int.)

V. Nellie Morley (Orchid World Int.)

Ascda. 'Bonanza' (Orchid World Int.)

Ascda. 'Sunburst' (Orchid World Int.)

V. Rothschildiana (Orchid World Int.)

Ascda. Cholburi (Orchid World Int.)

V. Miss Joaquin × Ascda. Yip Sum Wah (Orchid World Int.)

V. Sanderiana (alba) 'Constance' × Self (Orchid World Int.)

V. Southeast Beauty 'Nate Strachan' (Orchid World Int.)

Paphiopedilums

Paph. Farnmoore 'Rex'
(Courtesy Robert Jones,
Mt. Madonna Orchids)

Paph. Shapely 'Geisha'
× Dalla 'Viking' (Cour-
tesy Robert Jones, Mt.
Madonna Orchids)

Paph. Orchilla 'Chilton'
× Wendarrow (Courtesy
Robert Jones, Mt. Ma-
donna Orchids)

Paph. Divisidero Val ×
Vanesse (Courtesy Rob-
ert Jones, Mt. Madonna
Orchids)

Paph. Pueblo 'Animas'
(Courtesy Robert Jones,
Mt. Madonna Orchids)

Paph. Jim Iverson ×
Valwin Mt. Madonna
(Courtesy Robert Jones,
Mt. Madonna Orchids)

Paph. Bell O' Ireland
(Courtesy Robert Jones,
Mt. Madonna Orchids)

Paph. Paeony 'Regency'
× Carl Keyes 'Bion'
(Courtesy Robert Jones,
Mt. Madonna Orchids)

Paph. Niveum 'Snow
Dove' (Courtesy Robert
Jones, Mt. Madonna Or-
chids)

Species

Den. nobile (Author)

Onc. macranthum (Author)

Odm. grande (Author)

L. flava (Author)

L. anceps (Author)

C. guttata var. *leopoldii* (Author)

Brs. maculata (Author)

Epi. stamfordianum (Author)

L. purpurata (Author)

Miltonia and Cymbidium

Milt. Evergreen Joy Carmen 'Cole' (Beall Orchids)

Milt. Hudson Bay (Beall Orchids)

Milt. Bremen 'Anne' (Beall Orchids)

Milt. Goodhope Bay 'Raindrop' (Beall Orchids)

Milt. Bert Field Crimson Glow (Author)

Cym. Voodoo 'Gypsy Red' (standard) (Oak Hill Gardens)

Cym. Highland Mist 'Dillabirra' FCC/AOS (standard) (Oak Hill Gardens, Art Mueller)

Cym. Tommy 'Delight' (miniature) (Oak Hill Gardens, Art Mueller)

Cym. Ivy Fung 'Demke' (miniature) (Oak Hill Gardens, Hermann Pigors)

Part Two:
The Plants

Here are the orchids we grow today—the modern hybrids—with cultural advice to help you grow them successfully. I'll discuss the twelve most popular genera, emphasizing Cattleya and Phalaenopsis hybrids and the many new desirable varieties of Oncidium/Odontoglossum/Miltonia alliances. I'll also include the best of the species orchids grown today. These plants, too, have been hybridized within their own family to produce outstanding varieties.

I buy from most of the major orchid growers and generally purchase three- or four-year-old plants and then grow them on to the bloom stage. It is important to realize that growers do their own hybridizing either from seed or by meristem culture, and thus there are thousands of different varieties in each genus available from mail-order growers. It would be impossible to mention all plants from all growers, so I chose specific orchids I know and have tended. In choosing the orchids for this book I looked for these characteristics: easy culture, floriferousness, adaptability to temperature range, availability, and beauty. I also asked several orchid growers which plants they considered their "best," and I've included their selections along with my own. The specific varieties are mentioned here, of course, only as suggestions, not as endorsements of any plant. Send for catalogs and make your own personal choices.

This guide to culture is meant to be just that, a guide. It explains the basic techniques of growing modern, complex hybrids. Obviously some adjustment of culture may be necessary, depending on where you live.

The growing instructions in each genera are general; more specific information is included for each of the various categories of plants, such as red Cattleyas and art shade Cattleyas.

Plant varieties are listed by color—red, yellow, and so forth—so you can make selections easily. Most mail-order catalogs follow this format, so if you want a yellow Cattleya you will find varietal names under the section heading Yellow Cattleyas. If you want to know the parentage of a certain variety consult the *Addendum* volumes of *Sander's List of Orchid Hybrids* published by the Royal Horticultural Society (Vincent Square, London SWIP 2PE, England); these volumes are issued every five years and the cost in 1984 for the 1971-75 *Addendum* was £11.85 postpaid in the U.K. (£12.20 overseas) and for the 1976-80 *Addendum* it was £14.35 (£14.80 overseas). You can also order *Sander's List* from some orchid mail-order suppliers in the United States as well as from the American Orchid Society or from Twin Oaks Books of Lowell, Michigan.

Most of the orchid growers I've talked with prefer to grow plants both from seed and by meristem culture, as they believe this is the best way to ensure a complete stock. However, many tell me that their plants are predominantly mericlones, which assure them of plants with flowers the same color and size as the mother plant. Plants from seed do vary in color, size, and bloom time. An unbloomed seedling grown from seed will not always match the picture in the catalog, but a meristemmed plant is usually identical to the flower pictures. (Recently some reports have filtered down that there is an occasional exception to this rule, but more tests have to be done to determine how factual this information is.) When you buy plants, check the grower's catalogs; they generally specify whether the orchid is seed grown or propagated by meristem tissue.

Orchid Abbreviations

Alcra.	Aliceara	Cda.	Cochlioda
Ascda.	Ascocenda	Colm.	Colmanara
Asp.	Aspasia	Ctna.	Cattleytonia
B.	Brassavola	Cym.	Cymbidium
Bak.	Bakerara	Den.	Dendrobium
Bc.	Brassocattleya	Dgmra.	Degarmoara
Blc.	Brassolaeliocattleya	Dtps.	Doritaenopsis
Bllra.	Beallara	Epi.	Epidendrum
Bro.	Broughtonia	Fgtra.	Forgetara
Brs.	Brassia	L.	Laelia
Brsdm.	Brassidium	Lc.	Laeliocattleya
Burr.	Burrageara	McLna.	Maclellanara
Bwna.	Brownara	Milt.	Miltonia
C.	Cattleya	Mpsa.	Milpasia

Mtad.	Miltada	Paph.	Paphiopedilum
Mtdm.	Miltonidium	Phal.	Phalaenopsis
Mtssa.	Miltassia	Pot.	Potinara
Oda.	Odontioda	S.	Sophronitis
Odcdm.	Odontocidium	Slc.	Sophrolaeliocattleya
Odm.	Odontoglossum	V.	Vanda
Odtna.	Odontonia	Vuyl.	Vuylstekeara
Onc.	Oncidium	Wils.	Wilsonara

Award and Society Abbreviations

AM	Award of Merit	JOS	Japan Orchid Society
AOS	American Orchid Society	ODC	Orchid Digest Corporation
BM	Bronze Medal		
CBM	Certificate of Botanical Merit	RHS	Royal Horticultural Society
CCM	Certificate of Cultural Merit	RHT	Royal Horticultural Society of Thailand
CR	Certificate of Recognition	SFOS	South Florida Orchid Society
FCC	First Class Certificate	SM	Silver Medal
GM	Gold Medal	5WOC	Fifth World Orchid Conference
HCC	Highly Commended Certificate	7WOC	Seventh World Orchid Conference
HOS	Honolulu Orchid Society	8WOC	Eighth World Orchid Conference
JOGA	Japanese Orchid Growers Association	11WOC	Eleventh World Orchid Conference

5

Brassia

(*brass*-ee-ah)

The Brassias, often called spider orchids because of their very elongated sepals and petals, are epiphytes, native to Brazil and Peru, Mexico, Costa Rica, and Guatemala. They are generally large evergreen plants with pendant wands of fantastic flowers. When I first added them to my collection twenty years ago, they were considered curiosities. Today, they are favorite orchids because they hybridize so well with Odontoglossums and Oncidiums. There have also been some excellent crosses within the genera. Brassia 'Rex' (*Brs. verrucosa* × *Brs. gireoudiana*), a prime example of an incredibly beautiful cross, is very popular now, as are the Brassidiums (Brassia × Oncidium) hybrids. The Beall Co. has created many fine varieties.

The plants have plump pseudobulbs and resemble the rhizome-type Oncidiums in growth habit; leaves are dark green, and flower spikes are usually pendant, carrying many white or pale yellow flowers dotted with brown. Bloom season is late spring, with the peak at summer.

The species include *Brs. maculata*, perhaps the most popular, *Brs. caudata*, *Brs. gireoudiana*, and *Brs. longissima*.

Growing Conditions

Grow Brassias (species and hybrids) with Cattleyas; both kinds of plants enjoy some sun and warmth. In recent years Brassias have been classified as cool-growing plants (62°F at night) by some authorities, but I still would not subject Brassias to low temperatures. A daytime temperature of about 80°F is ideal.

Brassias like a buoyant atmosphere and do well with good humidity, perhaps needing a little more moisture in the air than Cattleyas—

Brassia (Photo by author)

about 40%. They revel in areas of good air circulation and will not do well in a stagnant atmosphere.

The plants are sensitive to location, so if they do not do well in one area, move them about until they find a place they like. A move of a few inches one way or the other can sometimes make a difference in growth.

Watering and Feeding

Brassias require plenty of water during growth, but in fall a slight drying out is beneficial to discourage foliage growth and help initiate flower spikes. Resume watering when spikes appear. During the winter, you can decrease watering, but never let the bulbs get so dry that they shrivel. If your home is so dry that you have to mist your plants, do it (to the pot or to the potting mixture) early in the morning so they will be dry by evening. Lingering moisture in the leaf axils can cause rot.

Brassias do not need, nor should they have, too much feeding. A moderate regime of, say, 30-20-10 twice a month is fine during spring and summer, with little or no food in the cold months.

Potting Mixes and Repotting

A general medium-grade fir bark is a fine medium for most Brassias. Add some charcoal chips and allow plants to crowd pots. Repot them only every second year; these plants resent root disturbance considerably. They are best grown in clay pots so that moisture can evaporate quickly. In plastic, the potting mix can get too wet, which may injure the roots.

Brassidium (Brsdm.) = Brassia (Brs.) × Oncidium (Onc.)

Bloom Season: Spring, Summer, Autumn

Brsdm. Edvah Loo 'Summer Fun' × Onc. Gold Coin Butte 'Yellow Monarch'	Golden yellow flowers; background amber with green spots and bars
Brs. Lanceana 'Vashon' × *Onc. macranthum* #1	Bright golden green to brown flowers with darker spots.
Brs. 'Rex' × *Onc. macranthum*	Greenish gold flowers splotched with bronze or amber
Brsdm. Golden Delicious × Onc. Gold Coin Butte	Bright golden flowers with tiger stripes of chocolate brown; brown color on the yellow lip
Brsdm. Golden Delicious × *Brs. verrucosa* 'July'	Green, gold, and brown flowers with yellow tips on the petals and sepals
Brsdm. Golden Delicious 'Golden Guinea' HCC/AOS × Onc. Gold Coin Butte 'Taxco'	Gold flowers with amber bars on the petals and sepals; yellow lip spotted with fine dark amber-brown spots
Brsdm. Klara Ahrnke 'Vashon' × Onc. Honolulu #1	Dark chocolate colors broken up by golden bars; yellow lip
Brsdm. Aloha 'Everglades' AM/AOS	Yellow lip and sepals; brown petals

70

Species

Bloom Season: Summer

Brs. caudata, a somewhat small plant, grows to 20 inches; it bears light green flowers, sometimes tinted yellow and spotted with dark brown on the lip.

Brs. gireoudiana, with flower scapes sometimes reaching 24 inches, has several yellow or greenish yellow flowers with a few blotches of dark brown. The most fragrant of the group and a showpiece, this large species blooms irregularly.

Brs. longissima has large pseudobulbs and long spikes of flowers. The flowers are large, to 7 inches or more, and are a beautiful eggshell-yellow with reddish-brown spots.

Brs. maculata produces six to twelve flowers with sepals about 4 inches long; petals are slightly shorter and greenish yellow spotted with brown, a white lip spreading and marked with brown or purple. This large Brassia grows to 30 inches.

Brs. verrucosa has the typical long sepals and petals, white marked greenish brown; plant grows large, to 30 inches with strap foliage.

6

Cattleya

(cat-*lay*-ah)

The Cattleya has come a long way since it was first seen by William Cattley in a shipment of tropical plants he received in England in 1819. Cattley, a horticulturist, did not recognize the plants and sent them to Dr. John Lindley, a well-known botanist, who declared them a new genus of orchids and named the genus after Cattley. By 1852, orchids had a great following, and when it was suggested to John

Cattleya (Photo by author)

Dominy, the manager of the orchid firm Veitch and Sons, that he and Dr. Jon Harris of Exeter should attempt to hybridize orchids, he leaped at the chance to produce a new Cattleya. With the doctor's help, Dominy developed the first orchid hybrid, Calanthe Dominyi *(Calanthe masuca × C. furcata).*

The plants were considered a sensation, and by the turn of the century some two hundred hybrids had been produced. Today, there are thousands upon thousands of hybrids, such is the popularity of the Cattleya orchid.

Widely distributed in natural habitats from Mexico to the Andes Mountains and the Brazilian forests, Cattleyas can tolerate a wide range of temperatures, from 55°F at night to 90°F or above during the day. Of all orchids, Cattleyas have been most hybridized, and the result is a treasure trove of beautifully colored flowers ranging from yellow to pink to green and almost all other colors, with contrasting lips of deep rose or red. The genus has been so extensively bred that the names read like a royal lineage. The intermarriages between Cattleyas and other genera (Laelia, Brassavola, Sophronitis, and many more) has produced plants far removed from the original Cattleya species of decades ago.

The colors of the new meristem art shade Cattleyas are exquisite. Bright apricot petals with orange lips are very popular, as are the

A specimen Cattleya with dozens of flowers. (Photo courtesy Armacost & Royston)

orange shades with contrasting lips. In the last few years the green Cattleya has come into its own. The handsome flowers with contrasting red-toned lips have come a long way since I first visited Dr. Clarence Schubert, an orchid hybridizer, in 1960 when he made this cross.

The extensive hybridizing and such mixed parentage have made it difficult to know exactly how to grow the Cattleyas. So many mixed marriages have truly produced better flowers—in form, in substance, in lasting quality, in adaptation to temperature—but they have also created cultural problems. Still, there are general guidelines; the ones mentioned here are based on actual growing of the plants under average conditions. The Cattleya community has so many hybrids that it is impossible to list them all. For simplicity, I have grouped the Cattleyas into art shades and color categories (as most catalogs do).

You have a wide choice of sizes in Cattleya plants. Recent extensive hybridizing has produced large, medium, and small plants, and even the miniature Cattleyas: Cattleytonias (Broughtonia × Cattleya) and Brownaras (Broughtonia × Cattleya × Diacrium). The standard Cattleya is about 30 inches tall; medium or art shade types grow to 20 inches, and the dwarf hybrids reach 14 inches or so. Miniatures grow to about 8 inches and bloom several times a year.

There are also true miniatures from nature, such as *C. citrina, C. walkerana* and others, growing 6 to 8 inches high. These are discussed in my book *Miniature Orchids to Grow and Show* (New York: W. W. Norton, 1981).

Growing Conditions

Cattleyas like moisture in the air; 20% to 30% relative humidity suits most varieties fine. If your home is very dry, there are ways to provide additional humidity for your plants (see Chapter 4).

For Cattleyas, as for most orchids, air circulation is vital; provide a free flow of air. A small electric fan operating at low speed keeps air moving when windows cannot be opened in a growing area. In the hot months, moving air cools plants even in sunny locations; thus if you provide air movement, you can let your plants have some sun. Without proper ventilation, however, the sun will scorch their leaves. During gray and cool winter days, stagnant air is an open invitation for fungus and rot to attack plants. Air movement keeps this hazard to a minimum.

Air circulating from the bottom of the pot is also important, to allow the Cattleya roots and the potting medium to dry properly.

View of a grower's Cattleya house. (Photo courtesy Armacost & Royston)

There are several ways to provide air from below the pot. You could make slatted redwood trays or trivets and place your plants on them. If you have a greenhouse, you can use slatted benches or wire cloth benches, which allow air to pass underneath the plant.

In their native habitat, Cattleyas grow mainly in treetops under a canopy of leaves, receiving dappled or filtered sunlight, not direct sun. Thus the ideal light is filtered, such as sunlight coming through a sheer curtain or through patterned window glass.

In the home, an east exposure is perfect for Cattleyas because it lets them receive the bright light of morning. A south area is fine, too; southern light is bright but somewhat warmer, which is suitable for Cattleyas. Avoid using a west window, however; heat can accumulate there, and the direct sunlight can burn foliage. Occasionally I have grown Cattleyas even at a north window with some success. Some hybrids have been crossed with species that demand less light (Sophronitis, for example). These plants can tolerate weak light better than other hybrids can, and will probably do well in a north window.

Watering and Feeding

Cattleyas need ample water, but they must never be drenched. More plants are killed by overwatering than by underwatering. If your plants are in 5-, 6-, or 7-inch pots, water them at least twice a week—three times a week during warm weather. Larger pots need not be watered as often because they retain moisture longer than small containers. In winter, when the weather is cool and the sun is not shining, water less often, but never let your plants become bone dry.

Water your Cattleya thoroughly and let the water drain from the medium. This may necessitate taking the plant to the sink, but scanty waterings can cause harm by wetting only a pocket of the medium and making roots work to find the moisture. Remember that most Cattleyas grow in trees in their native habitat and are freshened by periodic downpours but quickly dried off by the wind.

Ordinary tap water is fine. Let some buckets of water stand overnight to leach out chlorine if it is used in your water supply. Cold water can shock plants, so use tepid water; icy water on a very warm leaf can cause cells to burst within the leaf.

If you use bark or a bark mix as a medium, you must feed your plants regularly. Plants receive few nutrients from fir bark; indeed, the bark may rob the medium of nitrogen. I have been successful using a general all-purpose formula of 30-10-10 until late summer and then switching to a 10-30-20 food during fall and winter. Twice a year I also apply a light solution of Atlas Fish Emulsion. In general, I fertilize my Cattleyas four times a month when they are actively growing. This may be spring and summer or summer and fall, depending on the type of Cattleyas. Mix the plant food with water according to the directions on the package and apply it individually to each plant. Use enough so that it runs through the bark and wets it thoroughly.

Potting Mixes and Repotting

I have grown Cattleyas in osmunda, tree fern fiber, fir bark, charcoal, lava-rock pellets, and on occasion crushed brick. Today, I use a standard medium-grade fir bark. Occasionally, I mix in some lump charcoal. If you grow orchids in Florida, a tree fern fiber mix will probably be better for your plants than the straight bark mix generally used by California growers. Once you find a mix that works for your plants and produces good growth and healthy foliage, stick to it.

I generally use small pots for Cattleyas. I find that in pots over 7 inches, the bark holds water too long, and excess moisture can harm plant roots. In smaller pots, bark dries out quickly, usually within several hours, depending on the weather. I also believe that plants crowded in pots bloom better. Although there is no scientific evidence for this, it works for me; I get more bloom on crowded pots of Cattleyas than on those in large pots.

If you must use nonporous containers, such as the glazed ceramic ones, do so at your own risk. My experience potting plants directly into decorative pots has been bad. Evaporation of moisture is slow, growth is minimal, and plants suffer. If you want to use an attractive glazed container, simply slip a clay pot inside it.

Some people grow Cattleyas on pieces of bark, tree fern slabs, or cork, but this works only with the smaller Cattleya species such as *C. citrina* and *C. walkerana*. Most Cattleyas are too large and awkward in growth for satisfactory "mounted" potting.

I prefer clay pots for Cattleyas. Roots may cling to clay surfaces, but even if that happens, you can repot a mature Cattleya in a few minutes. If the clay pot has been used a few years, you may find that the orchid has attached many roots to the surface. Don't subject the roots to a tug-of-war. Simply break the pot with a sharp blow from a hammer. Then carefully remove the roots from the shards. Do this slowly and carefully, to avoid injuring the roots. Rarely can you simply tease a mature orchid from a clay pot; the roots take hold (as they should) to the pot's surfaces.

Once you have the plant out of its old container and the roots cleaned of decayed bark and debris, crumble away old potting medium with your fingers. Put some shards in the bottom of a fresh pot. Hold the plant in the center of the pot with one hand. With the other hand, scoop fresh bark in and around the plant. With the sides of your thumbs, pack the bark into place, pushing it down inside the pot, away from the plant, until the pot is filled to within one-half inch from the top. Then water the plant thoroughly once; let it dry a few days before giving it more water.

You should repot your Cattleyas every twelve or eighteen months. Do this no more than four weeks after the plants bloom. The timing is crucial; later, too many roots may have formed and may be injured in the repotting process, so keep close watch on your plants after their blooming times. Allow one inch between the new lead (new growth) and the edge of the fresh pot so the plant will have sufficient space in which to grow for a year or more.

Art Shade Cattleyas

The art shade Cattleyas are recent introductions that have great flair. Colors range from peach to apricot to orange to light pink and rust, with a myriad of shades between. Plants are somewhat small—purposely—compared with standard-sized white or lavender hybrids, and the breeders have fulfilled their goal: to produce a compact plant that is easy to handle and appropriate for small rooms. Most art shades bloom twice a year, and many can adjust to varying conditions. What more could we possibly ask for? One would have to go a long way to produce a better plant than Sophrolaeliocattleya Hazel Boyd 'Sunset' AM/AOS, which has apricot flowers with rose overtones in the sepals and petals—or Potinara Lakeland 'Britt,' with its exquisite orange flowers and ruby lips.

Within the art shade group there is a mixture of parentage: Sophronitis, Brassias, Laelias, Cattleyas. The combinations are mind-boggling, but the results are spectacular. Art shades give you a veritable treasure trove of color and a choice of bloom size, from 3 to 6 inches.

Generally, the keeping quality of the flowers is excellent—to about four weeks—and there are varieties for almost every season. The white and lavender Cattleya hybrids may be called glamorous, but the art shades are charming.

I grow these varieties, also called novelty crosses, in intermediate conditions of about 56°F minimum at night. I keep the plants shaded from summer sun but give them bright light in winter. The bark potting mix is kept evenly moist at all times, and feeding is done three times a month.

If you want to start to grow Cattleyas, the art shades are a fine group to try. Most plants adjust well to home temperatures, are compact in growth, bloom twice a year, and are not overly expensive. Many growers believe that in time this smaller orchid will outdistance larger varieties as the people's choice.

Art Shade Cattleya Hybrids
(amber, peach, apricot, pink, rust)

Bloom season: Mostly Autumn and Winter

Slc. Kauai Starbright 'Vi' × C. Chocolate Drop 'Kodama' CR/HOS, AM/AOS

Lc. Mary Ellen Carter

Bc. Lynn Gaine

Pot. Caesar's Head

Blc. Helen's Fortune

Blc. Bouton d'Or 'Lewis' AM/AOS × Blc. Minerva Manuel

Blc. Hawaiian Holiday

Slc. Naomi Kerns 'Fireball'

Blc. Malworth 'Orchidglade' FCC/AOS × Slc. George Hausermann

Blc. Bouton 'D' or 'Rainbow' SM/SFOS × Slc. Timmons

Lc. Chicanery × Blc. Orange Nuggett 'Kadaoka' HCC/AOS

L. Coronet × C. Mt. Shasta × Slc. Tickety Boo

Lc. Gold Digger 'Orchidglade's Mandarin' AM/AOS × Slc. Hazel Boyd 'Sunset' AM/AOS

Slc. Little Beamche × *Epi. corifolium*

Slc. Little Beamche 'Richella' HCC/AOS × Slc. Sunset Glow 'Richella'

Blc. Manu Flirt 'Chee' × Blc. Orange Nuggett 'Kadaoka' HCC/AOS

Slc. Orange Mist × C. Small World

Lc. Pixie Gold 'Muse' AM/AOS × Blc. Bouton 'D' or 'Lewis' AM/AOS

C. schillerana × Slc. Jewel Box 'Scheherazade' AM/AOS

L. tenebrosa × (*C. aclandiae* × C. Antigo)

Blc. Jewel Glo 'Hagardon'

Blc. Jane Sherouse 'Winefest'

Blc. Mellowglow 'Greenbriar' AM/AOS

Blc. Jane Sherouse 'Orange Delight'

Slc. Orient Amber 'Orchidglade' SM/8WOC

Slc. George Hausermann 'York' SM/JOGA

Slc. George Hausermann 'Carl' HCC/AOS

Slc. George Hausermann 'Ingrid'

Pot. Lakeland 'Britt'

Pot. Harlequin Peak 'Orange Princess'

Lc. Amber Glow 'Marion' AM/HOS

Lc. Amber Glow 'Mid Florida' FCC/AOS

Slc. California Apricot 'Orange Circle' HCC/AOS

Blc. Faye Miyamoto 'Pokai' AM/HOS

Lc. Autumn Symphony 'Cardinal' HCC/AOS

Slc. Hazel Boyd 'Apricot Glow'

Blc. Orange Nuggett 'Kadaoka'

Yellow Cattleyas

Yellow has always been a favorite garden flower color, and in orchids it is equally desirable. Yellow varieties are bright, charming, and blend well with almost any interior decor. Also, many of the yellow varieties have a pleasing fragrance. Some of the Cattleyas are yellow throughout (concolor), but many also have the traditional red lip, which is more dramatic.

In the intense hybridization of the yellow Cattleya, species such as C. luteola, C. flava, and C. citrina have been used extensively; these plants impart pure yellow and small flowers. Flowers 3 inches across appear on plants such as Laeliocattleya Golden Girl 'Miami' AM/AOS and Brassolaeliocattleya Arlene Finney 'Sunny.' However, there are a great many large yellow varieities with flowers up to 7 inches, such as in Blc. Frank Reyes 'Dee' and Blc. Hausermann's Yellow-Wood 'Chartreuse.'

Because of the intense hybridization, dozens of plants are available. However, not all have good flower substance. I have found some yellow Cattleyas weak in substance as compared to, say, the green varieties. Lasting quality also varies; those with Pacific Gold lineage can stay beautiful on the plant for five or six weeks. Because so many good yellow varieties are available, you can have plants for fall, winter, and spring, and even a few for summer bloom.

The yellows tend to grow well with routine Cattleya culture, but they need somewhat more light than the green or red varieties. Keep them somewhat more moist and feed them more liberally than the other Cattleyas.

It is difficult to single out superior yellows because there are so many very good ones, so this choice depends on your pocketbook. Some excellent yellows are available for as little as $30; others, such as Blc. Malworth 'Orchidglade' FCC/AOS/AM/RHS, may cost up to $100 (£40 in Britain).

My favorites are those with Amber Gold or Amber Glow heritage.

Most people find these varieties very satisfactory, if not overly large, and I never can keep enough of them in stock. Here are my choices from among the many fine-flowering yellow Cattleyas.

Yellow Cattleya Hybrids

Bloom Season: Summer, Autumn, Winter

Blc. Melinda Wheeler 'Halcyon' HCC/AOS × Blc. Golden Embers 'Chris' AM/AOS

Blc. Golden Embers 'Chris' AM/AOS × Blc. Malworth 'Orchidglade' FCC/AOS

Blc. Ethel DuPont 'Canary' × Jane Helton 'Orange Gem'

Lc. Amber Glow 'Kathleen' AM/HOS × Blc. Buttercup 'Robin'

Blc. Bouton 'D' or 'Rainbow' SM/SFOS × Blc. Buttercup 'Robin'

Blc. Fortune × Blc. Faye Miyamoto × Blc. Memoria Helen Brown 'Sweet Afton' AM/AOS

Blc. Memoria Helen Brown 'Sweet Afton' AM/AOS × Blc. Fortune 'Golden Throne' GM/8WOC, HCC/AOS

Slc. Rosemary Clooney 'Nanae' AM/AOS × C. aurantiaca

Slc. Tangerine Jewel × L. briegeri

Pot. Tapestry Peak 'Yellow' × Blc. Buttercup 'Robin'

Blc. Waikiki Gold 'Lea' CR/HOS × Blc. Faye Miyamoto 'Pokai' AM/AOS

Lc. Chine 'Bouton d'Or' × Lc. Ann Follis

Lc. S. J. Bracey 'Field' SM/SFOS × Lc. Edgard van Belle 'Mesbla'

Lc. S. J. Bracey 'Field' SM/SFOS × Lc. Chine 'Bouton d'Or'

Lc. Orglade's Goldburst

C. guttata 'Leopardiana' HCC/AOS × Slc. Kauai Starbright 'Vi'

Blc. Lorraine Malworth 'Orlando' AM/AOS × Blc. Golden Slippers 'Orchidglade'

Blc. Orglade's Memehune

Blc. Orglade's Yellow Jacket

Lc. Amber Glow 'Vibrant'

Lc. Alma Wichmann 'Summer Delight'

Blc. Golden Embers 'Chris' AM/AOS

Blc. Fortune 'Spellbound' HCC/AOS

Blc. Pacific Gold × Lc. Pixie Gold

Lc. Western Sunset 'Bronze Glow'

Blc. Arlene Finney 'Sunny'

Bc. Mount Hood × Lc. Fires of Spring

Pot. Fortune Teller 'Golden Morocco'

Blc. Memoria Helen Brown 'Showpiece' HCC/AOS

Blc. Arlene Finney 'Sun Ripe'

Blc. Oconto 'Yellow Pride'

Blc. Waikiki Gold 'Lea' HCC/AOS

Pot. Mount Yellowthorne 'Glencoe'

Blc. Lorraine Malworth 'Orlando' AM/AOS

Bk. Mount Triumph 'Wingtip' AM/AOS

Blc. Fortune 'Golden Throne' AM/AOS

Blc. Fortune 'Legacy'

Lc. Yung Hua 'Red Top'

Blc. Frank Reyes 'Dee'

Blc. Gold Country 'Mother Lode' HCC/AOS

Blc. Living Gold 'Camino Real' HCC/AOS

Pot. Fabled Peak 'Orchidglade'

Blc. Lorraine Malworth 'Orchidglade II' AM/AOS

Blc. Malworth 'Orchidglade' FCC/AOS AM/RHS, GM/8WOC

Blc. Mellow Gem 'Canary' BM/JOGA, PC/JOS HCC/AJOS

Red Cattleyas

People and nature have worked well together in raising the red Cattleya hybrids; these flowers demand attention. Within the red color range are various shades and tones of true red. For example, Sophrolaeliocattleya Jewel Box 'Dark Waters' has brilliant orange markings within the lip, Slc. Mae Hawkins 'Miya' HCC/AOS is true blood red, and Slc. Naomi Kerns 'Fireball' is, to my eye, a somewhat subtle red. The variations in color seem limitless, and it is hard to say whether Slc. Madge Fordyce 'Scarlet Orb' is any redder than Slc. Madge Fordyce 'Red Orb.'

Flower size differs, from somewhat small blossoms in Slc. Jewel Box 'Dark Waters' to large inflorescence such as Potinara Rebecca Merkel 'Sangre de Paloma.' Many of the red hybrids bloom twice a year in my shop, but some do not. Failure to bloom can be caused by cultural problems, but I think it is more often the habit of the plant itself.

Clues to growing the hybrid red orchids can be found in their heritage. In Sophronitis (S.) × Laelia (L.) × Cattleya (C.), the red color from the cool-growing miniature Sophronitis and Laelia species indicates that some coolness is necessary for the plants, and I have found this to be so. I keep my red hybrids 5° to 7°F cooler at night than Brassiocattleyas or Laeliocattleyas. In summer, I provide heavy shade for Sophrolaeliocattleya varieties with 40% shade cloth. Watering and feeding schedules remain the same as for other Cattleyas.

Generally, the red hybrids are more floriferous than, say, green hybrids, but the lasting quality—about three weeks under average conditions—does not compare to the five weeks or more common for green varieties. On one hand, although the hybridists have captured the alluring red color, on the other hand, some of the flower-lasting quality has been diminished.

Red hybrids cost more than lavender or white Cattleyas because reds are so much in demand. However, in time, as more red varieties enter the marketplace, prices should diminish slightly. Be prepared to pay $50 or more (£25 in Britain) for a mature good red. Here are some of the reds I've cultivated that proved to be excellent plants.

Red Cattleya Hybrids

Bloom Season: Autumn, Winter

Pot. Rebecca Merkel 'Denise Trowbridge' AM/AOS

Slc. Jewel Box 'Dark Waters' HCC/AOS

Slc. Falcon Westonbirt FCC/RHS

Slc. Riffe 'Burlingame' AM/AOS

Pot. Rebecca Merkel 'Sangre de Paloma' GM/SFOS

Slc. Naomi Kerns 'Fireball' AM/HOS

Slc. Madge Fordyce 'Red Orb' AM/JOS

Slc. Tropic Dawn 'Fire Flame' AM/AOS

Slc. Mae Hawkins 'Maya' HCC/AOS

Pot. Red Dip 'Ruby Jewel'

Pot. Amangi 'Orchidglade'

Lc. Autumn Symphony 'Copper' AM/AOS

Slc. Amberglow 'Fire Mountain' HCC/AOS

Blc. Gift 'Glory Gold'

Lc. Maria Ozzella 'Burgundy' HCC/ODC

Slc. Hazel Boyd 'Royal Scarlet' SM/JOGA, AM/AOS

C. Chocolate Drop × *Broughtonia sanguinea* 'Yellow Eyes'

Slc. Wendy's Valentine 'June'

Slc. Vallezac 'Billy Miles' AM/AOS

Green Cattleyas

Red may be some people's color preference in flowers, but others opt for the exotic green orchids that look dramatic in any setting. In 1960, when I visited Dr. Schubert at Clarelen Orchids in Wisconsin, he was breeding green Cattleyas. His work produced a handsome small green Cattleya with a purple lip. In the last two decades other growers have taken great strides in creating beautiful green orchids; for example, it is difficult to imagine a more beautiful flower than Brassolaeliocattleya Ports of Paradise 'Emerald Isle' FCC/AOS.

Many of the green varieties' heritage has some remnants of the species *Cattleya bicolor*, *C. guttata*, and *C. granulosa*, which helped contribute to the colors we now have (see the list of species at the end of this chapter). Some green varieties, such as Blc. Greenwich 'Elmhurst' AM/AOS, have somewhat small flowers (to 4 inches), but plants such as Blc. Pennsylvania Spring 'Orchidglade' bear large 6-inch flowers. Most green Cattleyas sport a purple or plum-colored lip, but there are all-green flowers, such as the Emerald Isle varieties.

For flower form and color and, most important, easy culture, I favor Laeliocattleya Kencolor × Lc. Irish Helen, which has great vigor. For lasting quality, my choice is the Emerald Isle varieties, whose flowers can last up to five weeks if plants are kept in a moderate temperature. Most green varieties bloom in fall or winter when color is scarce outside, making them especially desirable. Generally, all greens have excellent flower substance; they are heavy and crisp to the touch. However, because they are much sought-after, these varieties generally carry high prices. Expect to pay at least $50 (£30 in Britain) for a fine mature green orchid.

The heritage of green orchids indicates the need for a somewhat humid environment, but you can successfully grow these plants in average home temperatures of 58°F by night and 68° to 78°F during the day. Keep plants evenly moist but never overly wet, and maintain humidity at about 30%. I always shade green varieties in summer, using 30% shade cloth. Some of the greens carry *Brassavola digbyana* heritage, which would seem to indicate a need for high light, but a somewhat diffused light is best for these plants, too.

In general, the green orchids at the Garden District have outperformed the red varieties; the flowers have lasted longer, and the plants have been easy to grow with moderate care. Here are green types I highly recommend.

Green Cattleya Hybrids

Bloom Season: Variable

Blc. Envy × Blc. Verdant Venture 'Jax 2'

Lc. Ann Follis × Blc. Verdant Venture

Bc. Binosa × *Epi. phoeniceum*

B. digbyana 'Mrs. Chase' AM/AOS × Blc. Memoria Helen Brown 'Sweet Afton' AM/AOS

B. digbyana 'Mrs. Chase' AM/AOS × Blc. Lester McDonald 'Kelly' AM/AOS

Lc. Ann Follis × *L. xanthina*

Blc. Greenwich 'Green Meadows' × Blc. Pennsylvania Spring 'Orchidglade' SM/SFOS

Blc. Greenwich 'Elmhurst' AM/AOS

Lc. Kencolor × Lc. Irish Helen

Blc. Autumn Glow 'Green Goddess' HCC

Blc. Greenwich 'Frozen Daiquiri'

Blc. Cadmium Light 'Sweet Lime' AM/AOS

Blc. Ports of Paradise 'Emerald Isles' FCC/AOS

Lc. Ann Follis 'Green Goddess'

Blc. Greenwich 'Cover Girl' AM/AOS

Blc. Jewel Higdon 'Green Goddess' HCC/AOS

Blc. Esmeralda 'Heritage' AM/AOS

Blc. Pennsylvania Spring 'Orchidglade' SM/SFOS

Lavender and Purple Cattleyas

Just when I think the traditional lavender orchid, so representative of the family as a whole, is out of fashion, new varieties appear that spark a renaissance in this group. For example, Brassolaeliocattleya Bold Ruler 'Summer Magic' is a deep lavender that defies description. In fact, the color range is dazzling in this category; there are dozens of shades of lavender ranging from the old-fashioned pink to the newer deep shades. Laeliocattleya Drumbeat 'Heritage' HCC/AOS was the Cattleya prom orchid of grandma's day and is still quite popular, with its enormous 8- to 10-inch flowers and brilliant plum-colored lip. Potinara Fuchsia Fantasy 'Orchidglade' AM/AOS is one of the darker shades now available. Jones & Scully's latest catalog lists more than thirty-five lavender and purple orchid varieties, such is the scope of this category.

Most of the lavenders are somewhat large, and the majority have enormous flowers, which are so gaudy that some growers consider them vulgar. Many varieties are intensely fragrant, and generally flowers last well on the plant—up to five or six weeks.

The lavender Cattleyas are grown under the same conditions as the whites, with minimum night temperatures of 60°F and as much diffused sunlight as possible. However, I keep the plants evenly moist all year, never too wet or too dry. They are easy to grow and give a great deal of satisfaction for the care they require.

Most of the lavender varieties I have had experience with are strong growers, and bloom time stretches almost throughout the year, depending on the variety.

Lavender and Purple Cattleya Hybrids

Bloom Season: Variable

Lc. Harold Carlson × Lc. Princess Margaret × Blc. Debbie Dramm

Blc. Katherine Henby

Blc. Liese Pigors × *B. digbyana*

Blc. Liese Pigors × Lc. Bruno Alberts

Blc. Liese Pigors × Blc. Mem. Crispin Rosales

Blc. Susan Pigors

Bc. Marcella Koss × Lc. Irene Finney

Bc. Marcella Koss × Blc. Liese Pigors

Blc. Norman Merkel 'Natalie' AM/AOS × Blc. Bryce Canyon 'Splendiferous' AM/AOS

Lc. Irene Finney × Time-Life

Lc. Island Song × Stephen Oliver Fouraker 'Elmhurst' HCC/AOS

Lc. C. J. A. Carbone × Lc. Time-Life

Lc. John Mossman × C. J. A. Carbone

Lc. Stephen Oliver Fouraker 'Elmhurst' HCC/AOS × C. Enid alba

Blc. Mary Battle 'Martini' AM/AOS × Pot. Ronald Pallister 'Ron' AM/AOS

Pot. Ronald Pallister 'Ron' AM/AOS × Blc. Roslyn Reisman

Bc. Myrtle Beach

Blc. Dinsmore 'Perfection' FCC/AOS × Blc. Sylvia Fry 'Supreme' AM/AOS

Blc. Osiris 'Miami Shores' AM/AOS × Blc. Sylvia Fry 'Supreme' AM/AOS

Blc. Amy Wakasugi 'Orchidglade' AM/AOS × C. Nigrella 'Jungle Princess'

Lc. Adolph Hecker 'Lynn' AM/AOS × C. Nigrella 'Jungle Princess'

Bwna. Nora

Lc. George Baldwin 'Prolific'

Lc. Irene Finney 'York' AM/AOS

Lc. Drumbeat 'Heritage' HCC/AOS

Blc. Bryce Canyon 'Splendiferous' HCC/AOS

Blc. Ronald Hausermann 'Carl' AM/AOS

Slc. Brandywine 'Burgundy Beauty' AM/AOS

C. Irene Holquin 'Heather Ho'

Lc. Joseph Hampton 'Pageant'

Blc. Mt. Hood 'Lipstick' AM/AOS

Pot. Fuchsia Fantasy 'Orchidglade' AM/AOS

Blc. Norman's Bay 'Lucile' SM/SFOS/FCC/AOS/AM/JOS

Blc. Melinda Wheeler 'Halcyon' HCC/AOS

White and Semialba Cattleyas

The white Cattleyas, along with lavenders, have for years been the stock in trade of the cut flower florist trade. Cattleya Bow Bells (C. Edithiae × C. Suzanne Hye), a flower of regal proportions and immense beauty, was introduced in 1945. And although there has been much hybridization since then, C. Bow Bells is still today regarded as a superior plant. With *C. trianaei* heritage, this spring-flowering orchid is used as a parent in C. Gertrude Hausermann (Empress Bells × Bow Bells). Generally, the white Cattleyas have large flowers to 7 inches across, many to a scape, and the throat is usually marked with golden yellow—a pleasing combination. With white Cattleyas, hybridists have attained their goal in producing long-lasting, very large flowers with incredible keeping quality.

The white varieties with vibrantly colored lips—usually purple or red—called semialbas, have made their mark, too, as a hybridist's dream. These dramatic flowers may not appeal to everyone because they are large and gaudy, but they certainly can never be ignored when displayed. Laeliocattleya Stephen Oliver Fouraker × Lc. Mrs. Frederick Knollys in bloom is a breathtaking sight.

The white and semialba varieties are usually large plants, some to 40 inches, but smaller plants with smaller flowers have been introduced; C. Angelwalker 'Easter' AM/AOS is a prime example.

Most of the white and semialba Cattleyas are fragrant, some intensely so, and hybridizing has produced white varieties for practically every bloom season. For that one special place in the home, the dramatic impact of the size and flower proportion of the large white Cattleya is tough to beat.

I grow white Cattleyas somewhat warmer than most of their cousins (minimum 60°F at night) and with a good deal of diffused sunlight. I give them less water than the other Cattleyas, but never allow them to be bone dry; I keep the plants just barely moist in winter. I do feed the plants heavily during every season.

A few whites should be in every collection if for no other reason than for their keeping quality; some varieties have flowers that last six or seven weeks on the plant. Their elegance cannot be ignored in the world of orchids.

White Cattleya Hybrids

Bloom Season: Summer, Autumn, Winter

C. Marjorie Hausermann 'York' HCC/AOS

C. Bob Betts 'White Lightning'

C. Bob Betts 'Mont Millas'

C. Swingtime 'Villa Park'

C. Princess Bells 'Betty's Bouquet' AM/HOS

Lc. Jay Markell 'Sam Sharpe' AM/AOS-RHS

Lc. Zuiho 'Michi' AM/JOS

C. Angelwalker 'Easter' AM/AOS

C. General Japhet 'Caracas' SM/SFOS

C. Lucille Small 'Marshall' FCC/AOS

Bc. Mount Hood 'Mary' SM/SFOS, AM/AOS

Lc. Mount Juncal

Splash Petal and Flare Cattleyas

Sometimes I think the splash petals or flares—orchids with blotches of lavender, pink, or red against a white background—may be the hybridists' biggest mistake. Some people may consider them lovely, but to my eye they look artificial and this is one instance—and a rare one—where perhaps the zealous hybridists have gone overboard. These orchids have gaudy flowers that appeal to some people but do not get a second glance from others. You will either like or hate these orchids.

I have grown a few of the splash petals and generally find little difference between their culture and that for the large white or lavender Cattleyas. Most are floriferous, but the keeping quality of the flowers—about four weeks—cannot match that of some of the other colored Cattleyas.

Splash Petal and Flare Cattleya Hybrids

Bloom Season: Winter, Spring

Blc. Buttercup × Blc. Jane Helton × Blc. Waikiki Gold

Slc. Empress of Mercury 'Gwo-Luen' AM/AOS × Pot. Tapestry Peak 'Yellow'

Lc. Jane Warne 'Alii' AM/HOS × C. intermedia var. aquinii

Blc. Waikiki Gold × Blc. Malworth 'Orchidglade' FCC/AOS

Lc. Ecstasy 'Orchidglade' × Lc. Gay Feather 'Catamaran'

Lc. Butterfly Wings × Blc. Golden Sands 'Elizabeth Off' AM/AOS

Blc. Orglade's Moon Cheese

Bloom Season: Autumn, Winter

Lc. Chiou-Jye Chen 'Kitten Face'

Lc. Gila Wilderness 'Nippon Treasure' SM/JOGA, AM/AOS

Lc. Hong-Sie Chen 'Kaohslung Beauty'

Lc. Judy Small 'Delight' AM/AOS

C. Margaret Degenhardt 'Saturn'

Lc. Olga 'Chelsea' AM/RHS-AOS

Lc. Red Empress 'Wycliffe'

Blc. Don De Michaels 'Razzamatazz'

Lc. Aqui-Finn 'Villa Park'

Lc. Aqui-Finn 'Prism Magic'

Slc. Empress of Mercury 'Gwo Luen' AM/AOS

Blc. Aqui-Fin 'Splish Splash'

Blc. Goulds Glow 'Halcyon' AM/AOS

Blc. Beacon Mt. 'Gaiety' AM/AOS

Cattleytonias (Broughtonia × Cattleya)

Bloom Season: Variable, but usually Autumn through Spring

Ctna. Keith Roth 'Stephen Fouraker'

Bwna. Nora 'Waiomao'

Blc. Francis Hoshino × Ctna. Keith Roth

Slc. Naomi Kerns 'Fireball' AM/AOS × Ctna. Keith Roth

C. Chocolate Drop 'Kodama' AM/AOS, CR/HOS × Ctna. Keith Roth 'Richella'

Otaara Maile's Surprise

Lc. Wailea × *Broughtonia sanguinea* 'Stephen Fouraker'

Lc. Tropic Glow × Ctna. Keith Roth

Ctna. Sugar Plum

Ctna. Keith Roth 'Stephen Fouraker' × *Epi. cinnabarinum*

Blc. Oconee 'Mendonhall' AM/AOS × Ctna. Keith Roth 'Kodmam'

Blc. Waikiki Gold × *Brother sanguinea* 'alba'

Ctna. Keith Roth 'Stephen Fouraker' (subvariety Robsan) × *Sophronitis cernua*

Species

Bloom Season: Variable, but usually
Autumn through Spring

C. aclandiae produces one or two flowers, 4 inches across, olive green and blotched with brown-purple, the lip magenta with darker purple.

C. amethystoglossa is tall and floriferous, with exotic rose flowers spotted with magenta.

C. aurantiaca has beautiful 3-inch yellow flowers.

C. bicolor is tall (to 36 inches) and bears exquisite green and lavender flowers suffused with brown.

C. citrina is one of the few genera that bloom in pendant fashion. The cup-shaped flowers, 2 inches across, are bright yellow and very pretty.

C. dolosa has magenta flowers with a yellow disc in the lip.

C. forbesii makes a somewhat larger plant and carries two to five greenish yellow flowers, 3½ inches across; lips yellow, streaked with red on the inside.

C. guttata var. *leopoldii* is popular; some grow very tall. Huge clusters of flowers are bronze-spotted mahogany.

C. luteola is a small plant, 6 inches tall, with a 2-inch pale yellow flower with a white lip, sides streaked with purple.

C. nobilior has delicate rose-colored flowers, the inflorescence borne on a separate leafless stem. A most unusual species.

C. o'brieniana bears one to three large rose-colored flowers, front part of lip darker.

C. schillerana produces large dark rose-brown flowers 4 inches across, with a dark rose lip edged with pink. Blooms in late summer. When the pseudobulbs mature, give plants a bone-dry rest of five to seven weeks.

C. skinneri grows to about 30 inches and produces two to eight rose-purple flowers about 3 inches across.

Best of the Cattleyas

Pot. Rebecca Merkel 'Sangre de Paloma'	Large red
Slc. Naomi 'Fireball' AM/AOS	Brilliant red-orange

Slc. Jewel Box 'Dark Waters'	Fiery red; floriferous
Blc. Acapana 'Miles' HCC/AOS	Large yellow with ruffled orange lip
Lc. Hausermann's Summer Spectacular	Brilliant cerise flowers with purple lip, many blooms to a scape
Lc. Aqui-Finn 'Prism Magic'	Beautiful white and pink splash petal
Slc. Orient Amber 'Orchidglade' AM/8WOC	Lovely orange with ruffled red lip
Slc. George Hausermann 'Carol' HCC/AOS	Fine large orange with red lip
Lc. Amber Glow 'Vibrant'	Beautiful yellow with large red lip
Blc. Malworth 'Orchidglade' FCC/AOS	Brilliant yellow with heavily ruffled orange lip
Blc. Arlene Finney 'Sunny'	Bright clear yellow
Blc. Memoria Helen Brown 'Showpiece'	Chartreuse petals, yellow lip stained with burgundy
Blc. Oconto 'Yellow Pride'	Brilliant yellow with red-stained throat
Blc. Frank Reyes 'Dee'	Enormous yellow flowers with ruffled lip
Blc. Greenwich 'Elmhurst' AM/AOS	Fine green Cattleya with ruffled lip marked with dark burgundy
Lc. Kencolor × Lc. IrishHelen	Large green with burgundy lip
Blc. Ports of Paradise 'Emerald Isle' FCC/AOS	Finest chartreuse with large ruffled lip

Lc. Drumbeat 'Heritage' HCC/
   AOS

Beautiful large lavender with
large ruffled purple lip

Lc. Stephen Oliver Fouraker ×
   Lc. Mrs. Frederica Knollys

Handsome white with rose lip

C. Swingtime 'Villa Park'

Beautiful large white; lip
stained with yellow

7

Cymbidium

(sim-*bid*-ee-um)

Particularly in southern and northern California, Cymbidiums are grown extensively as outdoor plants. With large pseudobulbs and dark evergreen foliage, plants produce flamboyant displays of flowers on arching stems. They are highly desirable for decoration and color. Unfortunately, the standard plants are large—to 5 feet—and require a great deal of space. Recently, "miniature" Cymbidiums have been perfected, and these are better suited to home culture.

With over sixty species, Cymbidiums are found growing from the Himalayas to the coast of China and in Australia. They are not, as most orchids are, true epiphytes, but terrestrial plants. Flower spikes start in autumn and winter, andplants bloom from November until May.

Standard Cymbidiums are easy to grow only if you can give them the important cooling period in autumn so they can initiate flower spikes. A nighttime temperature of 45° to 50°F is necessary for about three to five weeks. If plants can be kept outside in late fall (temperatures are cool during this season in most climates), bloom is assured. Providing such cool temperatures indoors obviously would be impossible, unless you have an unheated room where plants could grow.

Cymbidiums enjoy a vast popularity because of their unique grassy foliage and long-lasting flowers. Most plants grown today are hybrids, and until recently these were almost entirely considered cool-growing plants. As mentioned, the standard Cymbidium is very large, and hardly a houseplant; it even takes up too much space in a greenhouse. *Cym. eburneum,* rarely seen now, was one of the parents of the first Cymbidium hybrid, crossed with *Cym. lowianum. Cym. eburneum* has excellent flower shape and fragrance, and *Cym. lowianum* contributed floriferousness and excellent keeping quality.

Cym. insigne, a species that grows in slightly warmer conditions than

Cymbidium (Photo by author)

most standard Cymbidiums, was used extensively in crossing; it supplied a color breakthrough in hybrids and more rounded bulbs and narrower leaves with erect spikes of flowers. Two important hybrids in Cymbidium history are Cym. Alexanderi 'Westonbirt' (*eburneum* × *lowianum* × *insigne*) and Cym. Paulesii 'Compte d'Hemptinne' (*lowianum* × *insigne*). These parents are still used in hybridization today.

When it was realized that there was a large market for a smaller Cymbidium, the miniatures entered the marketplace. What a vast impact they have had! These incredibly beautiful plants grow to about 24 inches and are manageable even in the average home. Furthermore, they do not require very cool periods to bear spikes as most standard hybrids do, and usually they can be grown along with Cattleyas. *Cym. pumilum,* a small species from southern China, is probably the most important plant in miniature Cymbidium history. It has produced many notable hybrids when used with standard Cymbidiums. *Cym. devonianum,* another miniature species, from northern India, is a frequent parent. Miniature hybrids have steadily gained popularity, and as I write this, these plants are outdistancing their larger cousins as favorite orchids.

However, the word "miniature" applied to these orchids is somewhat misleading, as the plants are small only by comparison to the standard Cymbidium height.

Growing Conditions

Cymbidiums like the best things in life: some dappled sunlight in the morning, a little less sun during the day, and shade from the very hot sun in late afternoon.

I grow standard Cymbidiums under a large rubber tree in my garden room. They are on the southeast side and do rather well in this situation. Come fall, I put the plants outdoors, where temperatures rarely go below 35°F and are usually about 48°F at night. If you grow these plants, find the coolest place in your growing area at night. Put the plants there and hope for the best.

Provide good air circulation indoors and keep humidity about 30% to 40%.

On occasional very cold nights, I protect the plants by placing a piece of burlap over sticks to form a tentlike structure. Such cold nights occur where I live about eight or nine times in the winter. When spikes appear, move the plants back into a warmer position—about 60°F at night. I grow miniatures with Cattleyas at 58°F at night and 78°F during the day, and the plants bloom fine.

Watering and Feeding

Watering Cymbidiums is generally routine; no special tricks are needed. It is best to water and then let the plants become dry before watering again. Give more water in the active growing season from late spring to early autumn and less water in late autumn and winter, but never let plants become bone dry. As with most plants, morning watering is better so plants are not too moist at night when temperatures fall. Avoid misting or spraying plants with water; this can cause more harm than good if water accumulates at the base of the bulbs.

Basically, Cymbidiums can be fed like most flowering houseplants: twice a month with 30-10-10 plant food during growing season. Feed 10-30-20 during the budding period. If you grow the plants in fir bark—many people use a soil mixture, which I'll explain below—Cymbidiums will require more frequent feeding.

Potting Mixes and Repotting

Although Cymbidiums are classified as terrestrials, they are not usually grown in soil. Some growers in various areas of the country offer a packaged Cymbidium mix, which is fine, but expensive. You can make your own inexpensive Cymbidium mix with equal parts of fine-grade fir bark, crushed gravel, and peat moss. You can modify this mix as you see fit, and perhaps add some humus. No matter what kind of mix you use, make sure that water flows freely through the medium and out the drain holes, leaving moist material inside the pot to feed the roots.

Cymbidiums do not want a mix that retains water too long. Excessive moisture can harm roots, so I use only clay pots for my plants. Water evaporates quickly through the sides of the pot. If you use plastic containers for Cymbidiums, water less often.

The question of when to repot Cymbidums arises often. Large pots become crowded, and people are apt to put off repotting the plants for several years. I have seen specimens at least twelve years old in enormous tubs. Once the mass of bulbs becomes so large, it is difficult to separate the plant properly. The dilemma with repotting Cymbidiums is that once you repot your plants, it will generally take them some time to rebloom again. These plants resent root disturbance more than any other orchid and generally will skip one even two years of blooming after being repotted. Is there any solution to this? Yes. Repot plants when they are crowded; do not wait until they are overgrown. Remember that any potting medium exhausts its nutrients in a short time, and even with supplemental feeding the plant has difficulty growing and blooming.

The best practice is to repot plants every two to three years. Let the medium dry out; this takes about a week. Then tap the sides of the pot against a workbench several times to loosen the root ball. Once the root ball is loose, grasp the older leaves with one hand, hold the pot with the other, and gently tease the plant from the container. Remember that the more gently you proceed, the less shock the plant will suffer. When you have extricated the plant from its pot, lightly tap the plant against the ground several times to loosen all old material; use a blunt-edged stick to poke away any remaining old mix.

Now return the plant to the work table and observe it, looking for natural divisions. You will see a clump of bulbs growing together. There will be a space between this clump and the next one. Separate the plant at these open spaces. Do not use a knife to cut the plant. Instead, grasp the clump of bulbs in one hand and the rest of the plant in the other. Gently keep loosening the tangle of roots, using a side-to-side and up-and-down motion. Eventually the plant will separate at a natural break. This method offers a good prospect of flowering despite the repotting. Do not water for a few days after you repot the division in fresh mix. Let the roots adjust, and then start watering scantily at first; increase water as days go by. Within a month apply routine watering.

This procedure may solve the problem of repotting a Cymbidium and still having bloom the following season. Then again, it may not, but it is certainly worth a try. It has worked for my plants most of the time, but in nature there is no guarantee.

Green Miniature Cymbidium (Cym.) Hybrids

Bloom Season: Winter, Spring

Peter Pan 'Greensleeves' HCC/AOS

Amesbury 'Green Magic'

King Arthur 'San Diego' AM/AOS

Pastoral 'Horizon'

Walu 'Emerald Jewel' AM/JOGA

Dag 'Charm'

Gerraint 'Malibu' HCC/AOS

Tum Thumb 'Calliope'

Tommy 'Delight'

Gareth 'Latangor' HCC/AOS

Red Miniature Cymbidium (Cym.) Hybrids

Bloom Season: Winter, Spring

Oriental Legend 'Lavender Lace'

Sweetheart

Pinafore 'Comet' AM/AOS

Fusilier 'Wild Rose'

Evening Star 'Pinkie'

Lady Bug 'Drum'

Leodogran 'Holiday'

Mini 'Lucifer'

Pipeta 'Brazil'

Ivy Fung 'Demke'

White Miniature Cymbidium (Cym.) Hybrids
Bloom Season: Winter

Show Girl 'Marion Miller'
Show Girl 'Claudia Rose'

Yellow Miniature Cymbidium (Cym.) Hybrids
Bloom Season: Winter, Spring

Gareth 'Latangor' HCC/AOS

Mary Pinchess 'Del Ray'

Cameliard 'St. Pats'

Nonna 'Golden Glades' AM/AOS

Bob Norton

Golden Land

Cameliard 'Sunshine'

Agnes Norton 'Show Off'

Mary Pinchess 'Sparkle'

Nonna 'Goldilocks'

Pat Ann 'Debbie' AM/AOS

Sylvia Miller 'Gold Cup'

Green Standard Cymbidium (Cym.) Hybrids
Bloom Season: Winter

Lagoon 'Braemar' FCC/AOS

Miretta 'Glory'

St. Patrick 'Shamrock' AM/AOS

Red Standard Cymbidium (Cym.) Hybrids

Bloom Season: Winter, Spring

Burgundian 'Chateaux'

Tapestry 'Red Glory'

Moonshot 'Easter Rose'

Valley Flower 'Cherry Ripe'

Voodoo 'Gypsy Red'

White Standard Cymbidium (Cym.) Hybrids

Bloom Season: Winter, Spring

Lillian Stewart 'Sundawn'

Mount Hood 'Coburg' HCC/AOS

Corchester

Lillian Stewart 'Royal Blush' AM/AOS

Lillian Stewart 'White Satin' AM/AOS

Highland Mist 'Dillabirra' FCC/AOS

Yellow Standard Cymbidium (Cym.) Hybrids

Bloom Season: Winter, Spring

Tiger Tail 'Canary'

York 'Glendessary' AM/AOS

Karachi 'Suez'

Sleeping Dream 'Tetragold' AM/AOS

Species

Bloom Season: Winter, Spring

Cym. aloifolium has dark green broad leaves, arching spikes of several flowers yellow suffused with purple.

Cym. eburneum, a somewhat small plant, has an erect flower spike with 3-inch flowers, white with a yellow band down the center. They are sweetly scented. This one grows best warm.

Cym. elegans blooming in winter and has yellow-ochre flowers.

Cym. finlaysonianum has yellowish green foliage and grows 36 inches tall. It bears dark red flowers with yellow margins and is a spring-blooming plant.

Cym. grandiflorum is big and showy with 5-inch blooms of yellowish green, striped red. It blooms in winter with many flowers.

Cym. lowianum has large 5-inch flowers. They are yellowish green suffused with brown shadings. A big plant, it sometimes reaches 6 feet.

8

Dendrobium

(den-*drobe*-ee-um)

The Dendrobiums (Phalaenopsis types) used in Hawaiian leis are *not* indicative of the many Dendrobiums grown. There has been a great deal of hybridization in the nobile group to produce exquisite flowers, but otherwise Dendrobiums have not yet come to their deserved popularity. With 1600 species, they are the second largest genera in *Orchidaceae*. The name Dendrobium is derived from the Greek and means "living on a tree."

The plants exhibit a vast variety of growth habit; some miniatures are only a few inches high while other Dendrobiums grow to 4 feet. Some are deciduous *(Den. superbum)*, others evergreen *(Den. phalaenopsis)*, and still others require a dry rest after growth is completed *(Den. chrysotoxum,* for example). Dendrobiums are classified as (1) evergreen: *Den. phalaenopsis,* (2) deciduous: *Den. nobile,* and (3) quasi-deciduous: *Den. aggregatum.* Care varies slightly within each group, but with careful cultivation you can grow these plants.

Perhaps *Den. phalaenopsis* and the nobile Dendrobiums are the most popular at this writing. In Hawaii *D. phalaenopsis* hybrids are grown commercially for their wands of white, lavender, or purple flowers, which have tremendous lasting qualities: up to six weeks. The nobile group, especially those perfected by Dr. Jiro Yamamoto, produce clusters of perhaps the most exquisitely colored orchids in the world. The new hybrids are stunning in bloom. Unfortunately, a great part of the year they are not blooming, and their bare bulbs do not make them a favorite houseplant. The pendant-type bloomers such as *Den. chrysotoxum, Den. dalhousieanum,* and *Den. thyrsiflorum* are spectacular in bloom, with beautiful white or yellow flowers. These plants may be partially deciduous, although most of my plants hold their leaves through the year.

No matter which Dendrobiums you grow (and I urge you to try

some), remember that the plants like small pots because in large containers they soon weaken. Grow Dendrobiums in 3-, 4- or 5-inch pots—even mature specimens. Some, such as *Den. aggregatum*, do well on wood slabs.

The Dendrobiums are true air plants, and more than most genera, these beauties need excellent air circulation and a buoyant atmosphere. They require bright light and some sun. When growth has matured—usually autumn—most deciduous Dendrobiums need a somewhat dry rest in a cool place (50°F) at night. Water only scantily during this time.

Growing Conditions

Specific growing conditions for such a diversified group of orchids are difficult to prescribe—and each group is grown somewhat differently from the others. I can only chronicle my conditions for Dendrobiums. I grow evergreen Dendrobiums with Cattleyas in intermediate temperatures with excellent ventilation and a humidity of about 30%.

Dendrobium (Photo by author)

I keep the deciduous types (nobile hybrids of Dr. Yamamoto) quite moist in summer, with a dry rest for about two months in late autumn; I reduce watering at this time and move the plants to a cool location of about 45°F at night. When buds show, I return the plants to the Cattleya area, and resume watering on a regular schedule.

The quasi-deciduous Dendrobiums such as *Den. aggregatum* grow all year at 58°F at night. I subject them to a slight drying out in late autumn, and after they flower, I let them rest again with little water until new growth starts, at which time I resume watering. I never move these plants to a cooler location; they resent new conditions.

Humidity is not a prime factor in Dendrobium cultivation; plants prosper in an average humidity of 20% to 30%. Too much humidity can harm these orchids, but good circulation of air is necessary to maintain healthy plants. In warm weather they must have a free flow of air at all times. Even in winter, use small fans to keep the air moving.

Watering and Feeding

Water evergreen Dendrobiums all year, providing ample moisture in warm months. The deciduous varieties require a strict resting period—very little if any water a few months before bloom time, and scanty watering again after blooming and until new growth starts, at which point you should resume watering. Keep the quasi-deciduous Dendrobiums evenly moist all year in the same manner as the evergreens, but never really soak or saturate them.

Of all my orchids, Dendrobiums receive the smallest amount of plant food. I feed evergreen types only during spring and summer, with 20-20-10 plant food about every third watering. Give deciduous Dendrobiums 10-30-10 plant food only in late summer and until buds show, and feed the quasi-deciduous plants only in the summer with 20-20-10 plant food.

Potting Mixes and Repotting

I use equal parts medium- and large-grade fir bark for most Dendrobiums. I repot the plants every eighteen months or two years. Again, small containers are the best for most varieties.

Dendrobium Phalaenopsis-Type Hybrids

Bloom Season: Mostly Summer

Den. Alice Queen — Yellow green, antelope-type flowers

Den. Betty Ho 'Sakata' — Clear canary yellow flowers of very heavy substance. Red-purple lip

Den. Circe 'Gail' AM/AOS-HOS-SMOS — Outstanding 4-inch blooms of royal purple. Blooms throughout the year

Den. Esther Zane Shigaki 'Butterfly' AM/AOS — Yellow flowers, contrasted by a deep red lip. Long-lasting sprays

Den. Floy Day 'Susan' AM/AOS — Excellent chartreuse flowers with a reddish brown lip

Den. Garnet Beauty 'Suzuki' — Very large deep burgundy flowers

Den. Hickam Deb 'Walcrest' AM/AOS — Finest phalaenopsis type flowers. Large, full, round reddish purple flowers

Den. Jacqueline Concert — Vigorous grower, bearing long, arching sprays of deep red-purple flowers

Den. Lim Then Hin 'Waipahu' AM/AOS — Dark reddish purple flowers, phalaenopsis type

Den. Walter Oumae — White flowers, long sprays, and ever-blooming

White Nobile Dendrobiums

Bloom Season: Winter, Spring

Den. Hoshimusume 'Canary'	Cream-colored petals and sepals, with a wide dark orange lip
Den. Hoshimusume 'Haming'	Creamy white flowers with petals and sepals tipped with light pink
Den. White Pony 'Akamatu' AM/AOS	Exceedingly large white flowers with good texture and form
Den. Yukidaruma 'King' AM/ AOS-JOS	Snow white flowers with a dark maroon throat
Den. Yuzuki 'Royal' CCM/AOS	Large creamy white flowers with a golden throat and reddish brown discs.

Splash Petal Nobile Dendrobiums

Bloom Season: Winter, Spring

Den. Christmas Chime 'Asuka' AM/AOS	Milky white flowers with purple tips; purplish brown in throat surrounded by deep yellow
Den. Gion 'Pink Lady' HCC/ AOS	Light-colored flower bordered with pink-purple; creamy yellow throat
Den. Happy Bride 'Orient'	Beautiful creamy white flowers, reddish purple on one-third of the petals
Den. Hoshimusume 'Smile'	Creamy white with hint of pink on tips; dark orange lip
Den. Momozono 'Princess'	Flowers with clear white centers, reddish purple borders on petals and sepals

Red–Lavender Nobile Dendrobiums

Bloom Season: Winter, Spring

Den. Andemos 'Mountain View' AM/AOS	Extra-large dark purple flowers with creamy white center
Den. Malones AM/AJOS	Large, beautifully shaped purple flowers with dark purple throat bordered by dark yellow
Den. Malones 'Brubon'	Bright reddish purple flowers, dark orange lip
Den. Malones 'Picola'	Dark reddish purple flowers with a dark orange throat and small reddish brown eyes in the lip
Den. Malones 'Saitomi'	Light reddish purple flowers with reddish brown throat
Den. Olympia 'Red King'	Very large thick-textured reddish purple flowers
Den. Oritopia 'Sanyo' HCC/ AOS	Dark ruby purple flowers with reddish brown throat
Den. Satellite 'Perfection'	Bright deep reddish purple flowers with dark orange throat
Den. Utopia 'Luster'	Flowers with large extra dark reddish violet sepals and petals; dark throat
Den. Utopia 'Messenger' FCC/ 9WOC, AM/AOS	Striking dark reddish purple flowers with dark yellow lip and reddish brown disc in the throat

Yellow Nobile Dendrobiums

Bloom Season: Winter, Spring

Den. Golden Blossom 'Kogane' AM/AOS — Delicate yellow flowers with a dark yellow lip

Den. Golden Blossom 'Lemon Heart' — Breathtaking bright yellow flowers with a golden yellow throat

Den. Golden Blossom 'Melody' — Petals and sepals orange-yellow with small purple disc on lip

Den. Golden Blossom 'Sunset' AM/AOS — The best of the yellows

Den. Golden Blossom 'Sweetheart' — Bright canary yellow flowers with a beautiful yellow lip

Den. Golden Talisman 'Yamabuki' HCC/AOS — Exquisite dark golden yellow flowers with reddish throat

Den. Hambühren Gold 'Eve' — Yellow flowers with greenish orange throat

Den. Pittero Gold 'Grace' — Outstanding orange yellow flowers with orange yellow lip

All Dendrobium Nobile hybrids are by Dr. Jiro Yamamoto.

Species

Bloom Season: Spring

Den. chrysotoxum grows 20 inches high and produces drooping apical spikes of many 2-inch golden yellow flowers in spring. It often blooms from old as well as new bulbs.

Den. aggregatum, a dwarf plant about 10 inches high, produces from the sides of the pseudobulbs pendant spikes covered with small, scented, vivid yellow flowers.

The evergreen cane-type plants include *Den. densiflorum, Den. thyrsiflorum,* and *Den. dalhousieanum;* there are others available. The apical leaves are broad and fleshy. Flowers are produced from the nodes at the top of the canes; they are set close together and perfectly arranged like a bunch of grapes, unbelievably pretty. These plants need dappled sunlight and even moisture throughout the year except just after flowering, when water can be somewhat reduced for about a month.

Repot these Dendrobiums every second year in fir bark in 4- or 5-inch pots. Home temperatures of 58° to 64°F at night in winter are adequate, with 72° to 80°F during the day. If you have trouble flowering the "Dendrobes," try resting them for about three weeks after growth has matured and then moving them closer to the window, where the 5° to 6°F drop in temperature may induce bud formation in winter. They produce their beautiful flowers in spring or early summer.

Den. dalhousieanum has flowers 5 inches across; they are tawny yellow, almost beige, and faintly shaded crimson.

Den. densiflorum is similar to others in the group but with somewhat deeper yellow flowers.

Den. thyrsiflorum has bunches of striking crystal white flowers with an orange lip.

The deciduous cane-type Dendrobiums, commonly called the nobiles, produce flowers in twos and threes from the nodes along the top of the bare canes. There are several species. Flowers are large and delicate, in shades of pink, lavender, and orange; a great many of the flowers are scented. In growth through the summer, these fine orchids need moisture and warmth, but when foliage has fully expanded with a solitary leaf instead of pairs of leaves, stop watering. At this time, usually October, move plants to an unheated area that has south light where the nighttime temperature is 48° to 55°F. Through the winter, while the leaves fall, do not water plants. When buds start to show in swellings along the nodes, move the plants back to a west exposure where the nighttime temperature is 58° to 64°F and resume waterings as buds increase in size. Repot every second year in 4- or 5-inch pots.

Den. fimbriatum sheds its foliage every second year. It is a pretty little plant that bears brilliant orange flowers.

Den. nobile, the most popular one, has white flowers tipped rose-purple, with a dark crimson blotch in the throat. There are many wonderful hybrids of this species, and color varies.

Den. pierardii produces 2-inch paper-thin flowers that are blush-white or pink and veined rose-purple. A very dependable plant.

Den. superbum produces a myriad of handsome large lilac-colored flowers from bare silver-hued canes. This species is extremely handsome and requires vertical growing space because canes sometimes reach 5 to 6 feet.

Den. wardianum, with 2-foot stems, has white flowers tipped purple with a yellow-stained lip. This plant is a shy bloomer.

The evergreen cane-type *Den. phalaenopsis* grow to about 2 feet and produce flowers on short stems from the top of the canes. *Den. veratrifolium*, known as the antelope orchid, is in this group but a rare species to fnd. Temperatures of 72° to 80°F with at least four hours of sun a day and abundant moisture are necessary for good flower production. The temperature should never drop below 70°F at night in winter.

Den. phalaenopsis produces many flowers, about 3 inches across, in a deep rose shaded magenta. There are many hybrids, so colors vary considerably.

Den. veratrifolium produces lovely, fragrant flowers, about 3 inches across.

Although the inflorescence of the other groups mentioned here last well on the plant (three to four weeks), the black-haired short-stemmed Dendrobiums are amazing for flower durability. Blossoms sometimes remain perfect for eight to eleven weeks. *Den. dearei, Den. formosum,* and *Den. jamesianum* are a few members of this group. Characterized by black-haired silvery stems, plants produce white flowers in apical clusters, the lips usually spotted yellow or red.

Any of this genus can be summered out of doors in direct sun once growth is well under way. Mealybugs may appear on leaves of the deciduous group, so inspect plants regularly.

9

Epidendrum
[Encyclia]

(*ep*-ah-*den*-drum, en-*sike*-lee-ya)

With a few notable exceptions (Epicattleyas—Epidendrum × Cattleya—and *Epi. atropurpureum* hybrids), the Epidendrums have not been used readily in hybridization and generally have fallen out of favor. Still, there are some excellent species in this plant family that deserve mention. Epidendrums—or Encyclia, as many are called now—represent a large and confusing family not clearly classified, and taxonomists are still wrestling with the genus.

From Central America, Mexico, and Brazil, these plants are terrestrial or epiphytic and quite varied in form, ranging from the reed-stemmed leafy *Epi. o'brienianum* types to the pseudobulb plants (*Epi. atropurpureum*, *Epi. aromaticum*, *Epi. vitellinum*, and others). Over a thousand species are known, and several in this genus are favorites of mine that I have grown for many, many years.

Generally, Epidendrums are easy to grow, but you must meet one requirement in raising the pseudobulb plants: do not keep plants too moist. The plants are free-flowering and produce many blooms in most varieties, and the majority can be grown successfully indoors.

Growing Conditions

The pseudobulb types, *Epi. aromaticum*, *E. atropurpureum*, *Epi. stamfordianum*, and *Epi. prismatocarpum*, for example, require a very buoyant atmosphere with free circulation of air. Even in winter a fan should be on to keep air moving. The plants like good humidity, about the same as Cattleyas (20% to 30%). These Epidendrums will tolerate a wide range of temperatures (78° to 85°F by day), and some coolness at night (to 58°F) will not hinder their growth.

The reed-stemmed Epidendrums, and these include the *Epi. o'brie-*

Epidendrum (Photo by author)

nianum and *Epi. radicans* species, on the other hand, like a quite humid and warm atmosphere; coolness may harm them. However, with these Epidendrums, air circulation is not critical as with others. Recently *Epi. pseudepidendrum*, with green and orange flowers, has been introduced, but I feel the flowers are not large or attractive and so hardly worth the space.

Epidendrums, known for constant blooming, require bright light with some sun (south or west exposure) and need average humidity to prosper. Too much moisture in the air can cause problems. Average home temperatures are fine (78°F by day, 65°F at night).

Watering and Feeding

The pseudobulb Epidendrums like a great deal of water while in growth but scanty waterings for about three weeks before their bloom time, and a decided, almost dry rest after blooming for about five to six weeks, or until you see new growth starting. Follow the same feeding schedule: give quite a bit during growth, say, three times a month, with 20-10-10 plant food, and then taper off before and after flowering.

Reed-stemmed varieties need water all year and can be fed quite heavily during the warm months. I use 20-20-10 for these plants.

Potting Mixes and Repotting

The pseudobulb plants require medium- to large-grade fir bark for potting; they need an open medium that dries quickly. Repot every two years or when the medium shows signs of decay. Follow Cymbidium potting procedures; handle plants carefully when removing them from the pot so the roots do not break. The reed-stemmed Epidendrums can tolerate a denser mix of fine-grade fir bark and can be repotted yearly. They are not temperamental about repotting.

Species

Bloom Season: Spring, Summer

Epi. aromaticum, about 12 inches tall, produces greenish white flowers powerfully but sweetly scented. *Epi. atropurpureum*, similar in habit, has brown and pink flowers with a red-striped lip. Both species bloom in early spring and are amenable to home temperatures of 58° to 64°F at night in winter and 70° to 78°F during the day.

Epi. vitellinum is a dwarf species about 8 inches tall, with brilliant small red flowers. This charming window plant should be placed close to the glass because it likes coolness, about 54° to 60°F at night.

Epi. stamfordianum and *Epi. prismatocarpum* represent the stemlike pseudobulb species similar in habit to Cattleya. They are large plants that grow slowly. The plants need filtered sunshine and do better potted slightly loose in osmunda or fir bark mixed with sphagnum. They need even moisture throughout the year, with perhaps a slight rest for a few weeks after flowering. They are slow to come back with new growth, so do not try to force them. Average home temperatures (around 70°F) suit these species.

Epi. prismatocarpum has bright yellow flowers blotched vivid purple. It is a real eye-catcher.

Epi. stamfordianum produces erect scapes of brilliant yellow flowers spotted red. The inflorescence is bunched at the top of the stem, lasts well, and is delightfully fragrant. This species produces its flower spike from near the base of the pseudobulb. It does best with a complete rest of five to seven weeks, with no water after flowering.

Epi. elegans produces flowers about 2 inches across. They are dark rose with a white lip streaked crimson.

Epi. nocturnum has 4-inch greenish white flowers that are especially fragrant at night. It likes slightly cool conditions.

Epi. o'brienianum has 1-inch flowers clustered at the top. As the lowest flowers fade, new ones appear at the top. There are many varieties, and colors range from pink to lavender to brick red. In climates that are mild year-round, this plant will do well outside in a garden, in a standard terrestrial compost.

For a start in this reed-stemmed group, try *Epi. o'brienianum*; it is available and inexpensive. The other species may be difficult to find.

10

Laelia

(*lay*-lee-ah)

As beautiful as Cattleyas are, Laelias hold their own with their cousins. These plants from Brazil and Mexico offer large flowers in handsome colors. Laelias are not cultivated extensively, but recently there has been a renaissance of these fine plants. With new hybridization of *L. purpurata*, many new hybrids have entered the market.

Laelia (Photo by author)

The plants date back to about 1850 and were popular in the ensuing years, although never very successfully cultivated then. There are two types of Laelias: the large pseudobulbs such as *L. tenebrosa* and *L. purpurata*, similar in habit to Cattleyas, and the dwarf Laelias represented by *L. milleri*, *L. pumila*, and *L. lundii*, for example (all used extensively in hybridization).

Generally, the smaller and charming Laelias are grown cool; the larger varieties do better in warmer temperatures and culture similar to that for Cattleyas.

Growing Conditions

Laelias like a buoyant, fresh atmosphere, average humidity of 20% to 30%, and minimum temperatures of 58°F at night and 75°F by day. They do not grow well in a stuffy, warm situation. The Laelias of Brazil, *L. crispa*, *L. perrinii*, *L. purpurata*, *L. tenebrosa*, *L. xanthina*, and *L. cinnabrosa*, for example, all do well in these conditions. The Mexican Laelias—represented by *L. anceps*, *L. gouldiana*, and *L. autumnalis*—like conditions somewhat cooler, by a few degrees on either end of the scale—minimum 52°F at night. The Mexican species enjoy a slight rest after vsbering and are carried somewhat dry. The Brazilian Laelias are best grown with even moisture all year.

Good ventilation is of prime importance to both types, and a free flow of air is necessary to keep these plants in good health. Sunlight is essential for all varieties; without it, bloom is sparse.

Watering and Feeding

Water Brazilian Laelias as you do Cattleyas. The Mexican species like the potting mix somewhat drier most of the year, and they need a slight dry rest after flowering. In summer, both types can tolerate large amounts of water if necessary, and the Brazilian cousins need it to prosper.

Laelias will adapt to the same feeding schedule as Cattleyas. It is a good idea to reduce feeding in all species in the dead of winter. At no time should these plants have excessive feeding, especially the pseudobulb types that store their own moisture and nutrients.

Potting Mixes and Repotting

Use large-grade fir bark for the larger species and medium- or small-grade bark for smaller plants. The Laelias must have almost perfect drainage or plants suffer considerably. Any lingering excess moisture is of little value to these fine plants. As a rule, repot only when necessary—when containers are very overcrowded. The plants tend to resent too much root disturbance and suffer a considerable setback after repotting—more so than most orchids.

Laelia Purpurata Hybrids

Bloom Season: Summer, Autumn

L. purpurata 'Cindarisa'	Yellow petals, red lip; 6-inch flowers
L. purpurata 'Maria Bonita'	Beautiful white petals, lip marked purple; flowers to 6 inches
L. purpurata 'Pedrevia'	Small flowers to 4 inches produced in abundance, mainly white with burgundy markings on lip
L. purpurata 'Doraci'	Exquisite large white flowers veined purple; purple lip

Species

Bloom Season: Variable

L. autumnalis grows to about 12 inches and produces an inflorescence 4 inches across, rose or pinkish purple, the lip white with a yellow ridge.

L. flava is a 10-inch plant with clusters of charming canary yellow flowers.

L. lundii is small, to 6 inches, with pink flowers, lip stained red.

L. milleri is small, to about 6 inches with vivid orange-red flowers. Very striking.

L. pumila, a 6-inch dwarf species, has pretty rose-purple flowers 2 inches across, large for the size of the plant. This is a good Laelia to start with.

L. purpurata grows to 40 inches with large white flowers and purple lip.

L. superbiens is a giant, 3 to 4 feet tall, with flower scapes 4 to 6 feet long, and is perhaps one of the most beautiful orchids grown. Large clusters of ten to fifteen flowers are brilliant rose streaked with crimson or purple.

L. tenebrosa is large with 6-inch flowers. Flowers are striking, brownish orange with large blush white lip streaked with burgundy.

11

Miltonia
[Miltoniopsis]

(mill-*tone*-ee-ah, mill-*tone*-ee-*op*-sis)

Whenever a Miltonia starts to flower in my shop, the plant is immediately bought. These somewhat small orchids with attractive grasslike leaves and flat pansy-shaped flowers always attract attention. Some Miltonias come from Costa Rica and Brazil—those with flattened pseudobulbs and almost yellow-green leaves that dictate warm conditions. The other group originates in the high regions of Columbia;

Miltonia (Photo by author)

these plants have dark green leaves and need cool growing conditions. They have now been put into a separate genus: Miltoniopsis.

With about twenty species, even out of flower the plants are attractive, and most produce blooms on and off for many weeks, one flower fading as another opens. Generally, the blossoms are sweetly scented—another plus for these orchids.

Miltonias have been extensively hybridized with other genera, producing astounding results (see Chapter 12 Odontoglossum, and Chapter 13 Oncidium). And Miltonia meristems have produced such rewarding varieties as Milt. Hamburg 'Red Velvet' and Milt. Storm, examples of nature and people working well together.

There is a certain charm and beauty to the Miltonias that make them very desirable in the home. The plants have not reached their zenith of popularity, but I think this will occur in due time.

Miltonias have also been bred with Aspasias to create Milpasia (Mpsa.), but at this writing no really outstanding varieties have surfaced. Miltonias have been crossed with Odontiodas, too, to produce Miltada (Mtad.). I have not seen any of these hybrids so can say nothing about them. However, I have grown many of the fine Miltonidiums and Miltassias, and here we find some remarkable flowering plants. (See list at the end of this chapter.)

Growing Conditions

Most books give strict temperatures for warm-growing and cool-growing types, but I have never grown my Miltonias in such stringent conditions. Basically, I grow them all in the same environment: 75°F by day and 60°F at night. If the cool types do not respond to this regime, I reduce their temperature at night by 5°F or so.

Bright diffused light is necessary to bring Miltonias into bloom; this can include a little sun (about two hours a day), except in midsummer when some shading is necessary. The plants normally prefer a location where they receive diffused light.

Growing to only about 24 inches, Miltonias are perfect houseplants if their few requirements are met: bright light, a temperate situation, and good air circulation. Once they are in bud, you can move the plants anywhere in your home for viewing; flowers generally last about three weeks.

Watering and Feeding

Unlike some orchids that need a drying-out period, Miltonias grow all year and must be kept evenly moist.

I think it important that Miltonias be watered individually by hand rather than by an overhead watering system. Lingering moisture at the base of the leaves causes rot; flowers are borne between leaves. A thorough watering is necessary: Really drench the plants in early morning, and let them dry out before night. I do not use tepid water for Miltonias because they do not react adversely to water too cool.

Most of the year I water my plants twice a week (most of the plants are in 4- or 5-inch pots), but in cloudy winter weather I reduce the watering schedule to, say, once a week. I do not mist the plants—again, because excess water can accumulate in leaf sheaths. Sometimes leaves turn yellow; this is a sign not of overwatering or underwatering but of an iron deficiency in the mix. Iron chelate applied once every two months can help remedy this problem.

Once every third month take Miltonias to the sink and leach out the dissolved toxic salts that have accumulated from food buildup. Let the water run through the potting medium for a few minutes.

The feeding program for Miltonias is vital because the plants get few nutrients from bark and cannot store food as the Cattleyas and Odontoglossums do. A balanced feed schedule is mandatory. Use Peters Orchid general food every third watering during most of the year, except in January and February. This program is effective if all other conditions are good—ventilation, humidity (20% to 30%) and bright filtered light. If the plants are not in these optimum conditions, do not feed as much.

If you have problems flowering Miltonias, add a tablespoon of bonemeal per 6-inch pot to the mix to encourage flower formation.

Potting Mixes and Repotting

The Miltonias as a group are considered epiphytes, which would indicate that the general bark potting mix should suit them fine. However, I have had my best Miltonias grow in a mixture of sand, peat moss, and fine-grade fir bark. The somewhat denser medium encourages better root growth with these fine-rooted plants.

Repot Miltonias every year; a decayed potting medium is harmful. The plants need excellent drainage, and decayed compacted mediums can thwart drainage and cause problems. Plastic pots may be a plus for some orchids, but I prefer small clay pots for Miltonias; they do not hold water as long as plastic, and the moisture evaporation through the walls is beneficial to the plant.

The repotting process is simple. Remove the plant from the old pot and select a container 1 inch larger. Do *not* use big pots for Miltonias. Crumble away all old mix. Prepare new pots with shards at the bottom and fill one-third with mix. Center the plant, and fill in and around it with new potting medium. Water the plant thoroughly, and then let it dry out for three to five days. Then resume the normal watering schedule.

Popular Miltonia Hybrids

Bloom Season: Summer, Autumn

Hanover 'Red Bird'

Franz Wichman

Petunia 'Red Admiral' HCC/AOS

Bert Field 'Crimson Glow'

Hamburg 'Dark Tower'

Evergreen Joy Carmen 'Cole'

Hudson Bay

Bremen 'Anne'

Goodhope Bay 'Raindrop'

Bert Field 'Ono' AM/AOS

Jean Sabourin 'Vulcan' AM/RHS

Emotion 'Red Breast'

Lycaena 'Stamperland' FCC/RHS

Miltassia (Mtssa.)—Miltonia (Milt.) × Brassia (Brs.)

Bloom Season: Summer

Milt. Minas Gerais 'Summer Day' × Brs. Edvah Loo	Amber and green flowers with yellow lips
Mtssa. Aztec	Rich yellow to cream sepals and petals with brown spots; creamy lip

Brs. Rex × Milt. Natal	Reddish flowers with lip fading to lavender
Mtssa. Olmec	Green flowers with amber-black spots and pinkish lips; some yellow with olive green bars; some green with dark amber-green spots
Brs. verrucosa × Milt. William Kirch 'Lipolani'	Brown to gold background spotted green to amber; labellum brick red and lightly spotted
Brs. verrucosa × Milt. schroederana 'Vashon' HCC/AOS	Chocolate brown flowers; light, spotted lip
Mtssa. Vino 'Mead' HCC/AOS × Brs. Rex Tahoma AM/AOS	Green spotted, reddish lipped flowers
Mtssa. Olmec 'Tiger Lily'	Yellow and brown barred flowers

Miltonidium (Mtdm.)—Miltonia (Milt.) × Oncidium (Onc.)

Bloom Season: Summer, Autumn

Mtdm. Ruth Coad #1 × Onc. Blanchettii	Dark brown flowers with dark gold markings
Milt. Red Pali × Onc. Honolulu #2	Red sepals and petals; lip white flushed pink with the same red color of the petals
Mtdm. Millicent Brown × Milt. Minas Gerais 'Summer Day'	Browns and tans; light yellow labella
Milt. Guanabara × *Onc. sphacelatum*	Metallic purple with darker crest

Milt. Endeavor × *Onc. sphacelatum*	Red-mahogany to chestnut brown flowers, sepals and petals tipped with yellow
Mtdm. Aztec Gold #1 × Mtdm. Lustre	Flowers dark brown to dark mahogany; golden markings and light yellowish lip
Mtdm. Aztec Gold #1 × *Onc. maculatum* 'Paulo' AM/AOS	Brown to dark mahogany flowers; yellow markings
Mtdm. Ruth Coad × Onc. Schilleranum	Dark amber brown flowers with yellow lips
Mtdm. Millicent Brown × Milt. William Kirch 'Lipolani'	Lavender, brown, and purplish tones; some white or pink markings

Species

Bloom Season: Summer, Autumn

Milt. candida produces 2- to 3-inch chestnut brown flowers tipped with yellow.

Milt. cuneata has same features as *Milt. candida.*

Milt. flavescens, from Brazil, has bright yellow flowers, lip marked yellow or white and blotched red-purple.

Milt. regnellii has 3-inch white flowers blotched with rose at the base.

Milt. roezlii bears two to five large white flowers, lip scalloped and stained with yellow and splashed with red.

Milt. spectabilis has solitary flowers with creamy white sepals and petals, broad rose-purple lip thinly edged with pale rose or white.

Milt. vexillaria has large white or rose flowers blotched with magenta.

12

Odontoglossum

(oh-*don*-toe-*gloss*-um)

These fine plants from the mountainous regions of Central and South America only recently have come into their own. Bearing exquisite star-shaped flowers in delicate shades of white and pink, the Odontoglossums have been extensively hybridized with Oncidium (Odontocidium), with Cochlioda (Odontioda), and with Miltonia (Odontonia). The hybridizing has produced some remarkable plants with long spikes of stunning flowers. On sight, these orchids almost take your breath away, they are so stunning in color combinations. At the end of this chapter are some of my favorites.

Odontoglossum (Photo by author)

Odontoglossums were hardly given the esteem they deserve when first brought to England over one hundred years ago; the custom then was to grow orchids—all orchids—in steamy, humid, and hot conditions. Obviously, Odontoglossums, because they are native to high altitudes and cool temperatures, perished by the score.

With large, plump pseudobulbs and grasslike leaves, the plants are evergreen, handsome all year, and when in bloom, stellar orchids.

Growing Conditions

Air circulation is vital for Odontoglossums because no matter how mixed their parentage, in nature the plants grow at considerable heights (4,000 to 6,000 feet) and are always subject to evening coolness and fresh air movement; hybrids still carry these proclivities. When supplied with a buoyant atmosphere and temperatures of about 50°F at night, Odontoglossums grow lavishly and require little care. The plants like bright light, but will tolerate low light areas in the home if necessary and still bloom. However, they will not accept a stagnant condition.

Place Odontoglossums in the coolest part of your home. Even during the winter months, keep a window open somewhere in the growing area. Do not allow a draft, but provide a flow of fresh air. If it is impossible to create such a fresh air situation, run a small electric fan at low speed most of the time. In warm weather, run a fan at low speed to cool foliage. On hot days, mist the foliage.

Because Odontoglossums like air, do not crowd plants. Allow enough space between them so air can circulate freely. Bottom ventilation is a definite plus: I grow my plants on slatted redwood trays.

Odontoglossums have been so hybridized that it is a moot question whether they still really need those very cool nights (45° to 50°F), but I grow the strains cool. Some of the newer hybrids—Vuylstekearas, for example—can tolerate higher temperatures. I grow most of my hybrid Odontoglossums at 50° to 55°F by night and 70° to 75°F by day. In very warm weather, when temperatures soar, I keep the air circulation at a maximum, and year-round I shade the plants against noonday sun.

The question of humidity with plants is always difficult, and it is especially so with the Odontoglossums. Some growers maintain that humidity must be high (60% plus). However, I have found that a humidity of, say, 20% to 30% causes no damage; indeed, it helps to prevent fungus and mildew. Too much humidity can at times be extremely detrimental to orchids from high altitudes. One way to determine the best humidity is to observe and keep a record for a year or more. See what humidity level does best for your plants and stick to it.

Watering and Feeding

Most orchids require watering year-round, but with Odontoglossums the best policy is to curtail watering somewhat in winter; most plants rest in the winter, and excessive moisture at the roots coupled with gray days can cause trouble. Give the plants a quasi-rest in winter by watering only every two weeks or so until early spring, when the plant itself will signal for more water by putting out new shoots and active roots. In winter, also decrease feeding to once every five weeks. When the new growth appears, increase watering to at least once a week. Light feeding every two to three weeks with Peters 30-10-10 plant food is beneficial, and remember to put plants in a sinkful of water for two hours once every six weeks to leach out excess toxic salts resulting from plant food.

In the summer, increase the watering schedule. Water as often as twice a week if there is a good circulation of air. Plants will grow quickly if all conditions are good, and by fall new growths should be ripened. Now slightly reduce the watering schedule to, say, once a week, but never let the plants become bone dry during this time.

Almost more than any other orchid group, Odontoglossums require the proper balance of temperature, air circulation, humidity, and water to prosper. If there is too much water and temperatures are not right, or if there is not enough moisture and air circulation is bad, the plants will do poorly. It may take you a while, but once you hit the proper proportions, your Odontoglossums will flourish.

At the Garden District, I rarely water from overhead because lingering moisture and cloudy days or too low temperatures can cause young growth or spikes to rot. The Odontoglossum spike appears between leaves, and accumulated moisture can create havoc, so I hand water each plant accordingly. This takes more time than overhead watering, but the results are better.

Potting Mixes and Repotting

I have found that for vigorous growth and twice-a-year blooming, Odontoglossums need repotting annually or at least every eighteen months. They cannot stay in the same pot as long as, say, Cattleyas. The plants resent a soggy old medium and like fresh bark; the compost must be open and free-draining. At the Garden District I successfully use a medium-grade fir bark mixed with a small portion of charcoal chips. This compost allows water to drain freely and air to circulate. Other composts include perlite-based volcanic rock mixtures and sphagnum moss in various proportions. But for vigorous growth, I prefer the bark and charcoal mixture.

Odontoglossums should be potted in either spring or fall; this coincides with their bloom season. If you are in doubt, repot about three weeks after flowering. To repot, trim away brown dead roots and then place the plant in a pot one size larger than the previous container. After potting, wet the compost thoroughly; this is vital so the bark does not take moisture from the roots. Put plants in shade until fresh new white roots develop. Water sparingly, to make roots seek moisture and thus build up a strong network of roots. Feed sparingly with a diluted soluble plant food, such as Peters 30-10-10. In about four to six weeks, you can resume regular waterings and move your plants to a somewhat brighter but not sunny place.

Note: Avoid time-released fertilizers, which may burn sensitive new roots.

Odontoglossum (Odm.) Hybrids

Bloom Season: Variable

Odm. crispum 'March Snow' × *triumphans*	Yellow or brown background with amber markings
Odm. Yukon Harbor 'Giant' × Jackie Gleason 'Pink Prospector'	Pink background with gold and lavender
Odm. Ocean Falls	Large white flowers
Odm. Red Cliff 'Fire N' Ice' × Gavotte 'Snow Storm'	Calico patterns of amber over an off-white background
Odm. Golden Ransom 'Pride of Vashon' AM/AOS × Gavotte 'Snow Storm'	Yellow flowers; some have amber spots
Odm. Yukon Harbor 'Giant' × Monarch Mountain 'Lavender Giant'	Lavender background with brown to maroon markings; most have yellow lip

Odm. Gavotte × Moselle 'Lyoth Gem'	Ivory to light yellow flowers
Odm. Crispum × Moselle 'Lyoth Imp'	Light yellow to canary yellow blooms
Odm. Golden Ransom 'Pride of Vashon'	Ruffled yellow beauty with red markings
Odm. Anneliese Rothenberger AM/AOS	Yellow-brown flowers; markings; outstanding

Also see Chapter 14, Complex Hybrids.

Odontioda (Oda.)—Odontoglossum (Odm.) × Cochlioda (Cda.)

Bloom Season: Summer, Autumn, Winter

Oda. Phryne × Oda. Feuerschein	Red and white flowers
Oda. Moliere 'Cyonis'	White-lavender flowers; blush pink suffusion
Oda. Chignik	Red markings on a pink and brown background
Oda. 'Jelly Roll'	Beautiful white with red markings

Odontonia (Odtna.)—Odontoglossum(Odm.) × Miltonia(Milt.)

Bloom Season: Summer, Autumn, Winter

Odtna. Debutante × Odm. Mount McKinley	Pink and lavender flowers marked with reddish and dark lavender spotting
Odtna. Debutante 'Everglades' AM/AOS	Bright red crest

130

Odontocidium(Odcdm.)—Odontoglossum (Odm.) × Oncidium (Onc.)

Bloom Season: Summer, Autumn, Winter

Onc. Lenalena × Odm. Mount Constance	Brown and white flowers
Odcdm. Unimak Island 'Golden Abundance' × Odm. McNabianum 'Spring Fancy'	Dark mahogany-brown cross
Odcdm. Costa Rica 'Vashon' × Onc. Clyde des Sain #1	Chocolate and yellow
Odcdm. Don Richardson 'Topaz' × Odm. Yukon Harbor 'Giant'	Gold spotted mahogany flowers with bright yellow lip
Odcdm. Costa Rica 'Vashon' × Onc. Clyde des Sain #1	Chocolate and yellow
Odcdm. Unimak Island 'Golden Abundance' × Odm. Golden Glacier 'Sunshine'	Brown and gold
Onc. maculatum 'Paulo' AM/AOS × Odm. Golden Glacier 'Sunshine'	Yellow and gold with brown markings
Odcdm. Tiger Hambühren	Yellow, brown flowers; striped; outstanding

Species

Bloom Season: Summer, Autumn

Odm. citrosmum is a pendulous variety that has fragrant and frilly white flowers splotched with light pink or purple at the base of the lip. This fine orchid requires 50° to 56°F at night in winter.

Odm. grande (Rossioglossum grande), commonly called the tiger orchid, has large yellow flowers, six inches across, and barred with brown.

Odm. pulchellum is a small plant, about 14 inches tall, with tiny white flowers delightfully scented.

Odm. rossii is a dwarf plant to about 8 inches and produces small white or rose flowers spotted maroon and with a broad scalloped lip.

Odm. uro-skinneri is a handsome plant. The large flowers have greenish sepals and petals marked with rich chestnut brown. The heart-shaped lip is pink, broad, and marbled white. A very spectacular orchid.

13

Oncidium

(on-*sid*-ee-um)

The Oncidiums are a large, diversified group of plants with different growth habits, but the majority have one common characteristic: yellow flowers marked with brown. From varied parts of Brazil, the plants were imported into England on a large scale in the late 1800s, but most perished because growers lacked cultural knowledge. The plants have varied types of growth: a climbing rhizome habit, as in *Onc. sphacelatum,* and a sympodial horizontal growth habit, as in *Onc. luridum.* Some, such as *Onc. lanceanum,* have no pseudobulbs, while others do, and a few have an almost vandaceous growth pattern, such as *Onc. triquetrum.* In all, it is a confusing genus, and no doubt in time there will be subdivisions.

The most popular species is perhaps *Onc. splendidum,* with solitary cactuslike leaves to 20 inches and erect flower scapes of yellow and brown flowers—quite handsome. *Onc. ampliatum,* the turtle orchid, so named because the pseudobulbs are large and turtlelike, has fleshy leaves and a wiry stem with hundreds of $1/2$-inch yellow and brown flowers. *Onc. flexuosum* produces long, wiry stems to 4 feet, crowded with small blossoms, and the unusual *Onc. papilio,* the butterfly orchid, which caused a sensation in England when first discovered a hundred years ago or so, is still grown today. The brown and yellow flowers are three inches or more, resemble a butterfly, and as one flower fades, another will bloom on the wiry stem.

Oncidiums have been bred extensively with Odontoglossums and Miltonias, and the results have been astonishing. (See Chapter 14, Complex Hybrids, and Chapter 12, Odontoglossum).

In recent years the equitant Oncidiums have become popular; these small plants, to 3 inches have fan-shaped leaf growth and produce small but beautiful flowers in an array of colors. The blooms are on wiry stems; do not cut the stems until they turn straw brown, as these

Oncidium (Photo by author)

diminutive beauties produce secondary spikes of flowers so the grower can have color at the window for many months through spring to summer. Orchid World International, Inc., of Miami, Florida, has done an outstanding job of bringing these charming plants to the attention of everyone.

Plants are inexpensive, and there are dozens of varieties; my favorites are Onc. Golden Sunset 'Fumi,' Onc. Wilbur Elizabeth AM/AOS, Puck 'Richella,' and Onc. Potpourri.

Growing Conditions

As diversified as the plants are, Oncidiums are not difficult to grow. Some, like *Onc. ornithorhynchum,* need coolness, but many prosper with Cattleyas—in moderate warmth. Under cultivation, the Oncidiums need much less light than growers once believed. They grow very well with bright light or some dappled sunshine. Sun is not mandatory, as it is for Vandas, for example. Bloom may be less then optimum for most varieties, but don't rule out Oncidiums just because you do not have bright sunlight. The succulent-leaf types such as *Onc. lanceanum* and *Onc. splendidum* need bright light; those with pseudobulbs, such as *Onc. sphacelatum* and *Onc. flexuosum*, thrive in dappled sunlight, and I have had *Onc. sarcodes*, with its charming bright yellow and brown flowers, bloom at a north window.

The temperature requirements of the Oncidiums vary. A range of 54° to 58°F at night suits the cooler plants, such as *Onc. ornithorhynchum* and *Onc. macranthum*. For the so-called intermediate or warm growers, 58°F at night is adequate.

As with many orchids, and perhaps more so for Oncidiums, avoid great fluctuations of temperature. A drastic sudden drop in temperature harms many Oncidiums, so whenever possible keep the nighttime and daytime temperature difference to 10° to 12°.

Most Oncidiums do not require excessive humidity—20% to 30% is fine. In nature, Oncidiums grow from sea level to 12,000 feet in the Peruvian mountains. The plants in general show a great ability to adjust to their environment when necessary, but this takes time— perhaps three months or more—so never give up on these fine orchids.

A buoyant atmosphere is necessary; Oncidiums need a good circulation of air to do well. Even in winter keep air moving in the growing area.

Watering and Feeding

Water warm-growing varieties frequently in spring and summer. Most plants can tolerate a great deal of water if ventilation is adequate. Cool growers can be somewhat less moist, but never let them dry out completely. Any excessive drying out of Oncidiums harms them: growth will be weak and flowers sparse.

The best rule of thumb for Oncidium feeding is to feed plants moderately all year; I apply 20-20-10 plant food three times a month except in midwinter, when I reduce feeding to once a month.

Potting Mixes and Repotting

Use equal parts of fine- and medium-grade fir bark for Oncidiums, and add a handful of charcoal chips to a 6-inch pot. I have found that growing Oncidiums on bark or cork mounts really does not work well because the mounts dry out too quickly. I have lost too many plants using this procedure.

Plastic pots are satisfactory for these orchids, although for the larger varieties, clay is better; big plants topple over in plastic containers. Use small pots for Oncidiums; I have noticed that it takes plants longer to flower in large pots. As with so many orchids, tight quarters seem to encourage flower production.

Repot these orchids every eighteen months, or whenever the bark appears deteriorated. The procedure for repotting is the same as for most orchids, as described in Chapter 4.

Oncidium Hybrids

Lenalena 'Vashon' × Honolulu	Gold medium-sized flowers with dark mahogany sepals and petals flecked with gold
Waiomao Gold × Ella 'Flambeau'	Yellow and brown petals and sepals; yellow lip
Copper Falls	Cascading brown mahogany flowers; butter yellow lip
Kutoo #2 × Jamie Sutton #1	Small burgundy and burnished brown flowers
Lenalena 'Vashon' × *Onc. sphacelatum*	Purple-red flowers with white tips on petals and sepals; whitish lip
Kutto #1 × *Onc. sarcodes* #1	Flowers chocolate and mahogany red with yellow markings
Memoria Pepito de Restrepo 'Vashon' × *Onc. splendidum* 'Supers'	Yellow and gold flowers
Kutoo × Gold Coin Butte 'Sunshine'	Golden yellow flowers with amber-brown splotching
Maui Gold 'July'	Chocolate brown petals and sepals with fine yellow line on the edges

Kutoo × *Onc. sphacelatum*	Chestnut brown to mahogany flowers barred yellow; yellow and red-brown toned lips
Onc. tigrinum	Yellow and gold flowers on branched sprays

Also see Chapter 14, Complex Hybrids.

Species

Bloom Season: Mostly Spring, Summer

Onc. ampliatum, with turtle-shaped pseudobulbs, has small spray-type yellow and red-brown flowers. When flowers fade, the plant sometimes produces a second scape if the same spike is cut below the last node.

Onc. leucochilum has yellow-green flowers barred with brown.

Onc. macranthum has sprays of lovely bright yellow flowers on wiry spikes.

Onc. ornithorhynchum grows about 14 inches tall and has hundreds of tiny lilac flowers. A very fine plant that needs semishade and cool nighttime temperatures of 52° to 58°F in winter.

Onc. sarcodes is compact, 16 inches tall, and produces pretty scalloped yellow and chestnut-brown flowers.

Onc. splendidum, the most commonly grown, has solitary cactuslike leaves 12 inches long, vibrant yellow flowers barred with brown, and a large and broad yellow lip.

Onc. wentworthianum bears flowers about an inch across, yellow blotched with brown. *Onc. sarcodes*, *Onc. splendidum*, and *Onc. wentworthianum* are excellent for window culture since they do not require as much direct sun as most in the genus.

14

Complex Hybrids: Odontoglossum, Oncidium, Miltonia

I originally intended to include the complex hybrid plants within their appropriate genera, but these new orchids are so exceptional and promising that they require a discussion of their own. Also, the mixed marriages have produced varied sets of cultural rules for the plants.

The complex crosses comprise a wide variety of plants; basically they are produced from two or more genera. The reason for the cross-breeding is to produce plants that grow easily in many environments. The crosses also have resulted in improved flower size, more appealing patterns, and a better habit of inflorescence than the individual species or hybrids of the parental genera. In other words, they are "better" plants.

When I first opened the Garden District orchid shop, I purchased many Odontoglossum and Oncidium multigeneric hybrids from the Beall Company of Vashon Island, Washington, which excels in the breeding and production of these fine plants. The hybrids are a boon for plant enthusiasts.

The flamboyant beauty of these mixed-genera orchids cannot be ignored, even by a non–flower lover. The plants' long wands of beautiful mutlicolored flowers always create a sensation. And many varieties bloom two, sometimes three, times a year. Most tolerate cool conditions if necessary, and many seem to grow by themselves if watered and fed properly.

The Aliceares offer a kaleidoscope of colors in small- to medium-sized flowers, with yellow, gold, lavender, and darker shades of red predominating; sepals and petals are pointed and the flowers star-shaped. Alcra. Sunday Best 'Augie' HCC/AOS is a prime example of lavender hues. Alcra. Maury Island 'Vashon' AM/AOS, registered by the Beall Company in 1975, offers exquisite yellow color in the sepals, and petals are marked with brown as is the patterned lip. Alcra. Dorothy Oka 'Tadoa Himori' HCC/AOS is a brilliant study in yellow and dark brown. Alicearas' parentage includes an array of Oncidium species: *Onc. marshallianum, Onc. powellii, Onc. hastatum, Onc. leucochilum,* and others. Each has contributed something to the present-day hybrids.

The Beallaras bred at the Beall Company are white, pink, or yellow and shades in between—a quadrigeneric hybrid of Brassia, Cochlioda, Miltonia, and Odontoglossum. Beallara Tahoma Glacier (Miltonia Cartagena × Odontioda Alaskan Sunset) is a striking white of heavy substance with red spots.

Burragearas (Cochlioda × Miltonia × Odontoglossum × Oncidium) are still another grouping of brilliantly colored flowers, primarily red. Many of these plants, created mainly by W. W. G. Moir, are exceptional, and recent developments have brought forth the beautiful Burrageara Living Fire, bred by Dr. Howard Liebman, which has become so prominent in ongoing development of this complex of plants. When you add Aspasia heritage and omit the Oncidium lineage, you have the complex hybrid Blackara, which should add more markings and darker colors to flowers.

Degarmoaras, trigeneric crosses of Miltonia × Brassia × Odontoglossum, show exceptional promise in a variety of dark-hued, mainly purple-lavender colors, and Colmanaras (Miltonia × Odontoglossom × Oncidium), with somewhat small but beautifully marked flowers, cannot be ignored either. Of all the complex crosses, perhaps the most popular and most beautiful is the superb Maclellanara Pagan Lovesong; the first cross registered in this genus was Odontocidium Tiger Butter × *Brassia verrucosa.* Progeny of these plants have won many awards, and the striking brown and yellow star-shaped flowers are a joy to see. When I had these plants, they stopped traffic at the shop.

The Vuylstekearas took the orchid world by storm when they appeared on the scene. Here was a beautiful flower combining red and white into a tapestry of beauty. Furthermore, the plants were easily cultivated and the flowers long-lasting. Healthy specimens produced dozens of flowers. This trigeneric cross of Cochlioda × Miltonia × Odontoglossum is still one of the most popular plants at the Garden District. It will be interesting to see further developments in this particular line of breeding.

Not to be forgotten in this parade of highly bred plant complexes are the Wilsonaras. I have had many of these beauties in the shop, and the long wands of colorful flowers run the gambit from yellow to orange to brown. These exceedingly fine plants sometimes bloom for me three times a year!

Most of my complex crosses have come from the Beall Company, and I have grown several of them on to specimen size. Their culture is relatively simple: intermediate to cool temperatures at night (55°F) and even moisture all year, except in winter, when plants can be grown somewhat on the dry side. These orchids revel in diffused light and seem always to be growing. I feed them heavily in spring, but usually during the rest of the year I adopt a moderate feeding program of two or three weak applications a month.

Multigeneric Crosses
Aliceara (Alcra.)—Brassia (Brs.) × Miltonia (Milt.) × Oncidium (Onc.)
Bloom Season: Spring, Summer, Autumn

Mtssa. Vino 'Mead' HCC/AOS × *Onc. crispum* Grandiflorum — Dark tones of shiny brown-mahogany with some gold markings

Mtssa. Charles M. Fitch × Onc. Ella 'Flambeau' — Broad yellow labellum with a few brown spots; sepals and petals barred amber over gold

Mtssa. Vino 'Mead' HCC/AOS × Onc. Schilleranum — Yellow and gold florets with a broad labellum

Mtssa. Vino 'Mead' HCC/AOS × Onc. Fallens 'Vashon' — Golden yellow with dark markings

Mtssa. Citron × Onc. Gold Coin Butte 'Yucatan' — Lemony gold with spotting on the petals; amber lip

Brsdm. Klara Ahrnke × Milt. Rio × Cogniauxiae — Dark amber tones with black chocolate overriding golden bars

Mtssa. Vino 'Mead' HCC/AOS × Onc. Liebmanii — Green-gold background; lip flared and curved in and up at tip

Mtssa. Charles M. Fitch × *Onc. tigrinum*	Yellow to greenish and bronze; heavy spotting on petals and sepals
Mtssa. Cartagena × Onc. Waiomao Gold	Lightly spotted yellow flowers with a large yellow labellum
Mtssa. Vino 'Mead' HCC/AOS × Onc. Waiomao Gold	Overall coloring in darker shades of glowing gold to amber
Mtssa. Mossy Knoll 'May' × Onc. Honolulu #3	Dark brown overlaid with fine bright golden lines; tip purplish with greenish brown spots cascading down over white
Alcra. Waiomao 'Tahitian Dancer' × Milt. Matto Grosso 'Summer Night'	Amber spots on upper part; golden sepals and petals are zebra-striped with darker colors
Mtssa. Vino 'Mead' HCC/AOS × Onc. Nona 'Davieland' SM/SFOS	Beautiful broad labella with amber spots; amber spots on base of petals and sepals
Mtssa. Citron × *Onc. sarcodes* #1	Brown and gold spotting
Mtssa. Charles M. Fitch × *Onc. crispum* 'Everglades' AM/AOS	Yellow to beige with dark brown bars and spots
Alcra. Pacesetter × Onc. Honolulu	Dark chocolate brown flower with gold markings
Mtssa. Vino 'Mead' HCC/AOS × Onc. Ella 'Flambeau'	Yellow with bright golden amber spots
Mtssa. Citron × Onc. Ella 'Flambeau'	Yellow and lemony golds with amber markings
Mtssa. Vino 'Mead' HCC/AOS × *Onc. crispum* #1	Shiny brown-mahogany with some gold markings
Milt. Festiva × *Brs. verrucosa* × *Onc. oblongatum*	Yellow tones marked in dark brown

Bakerara (Bak.)—Brassia (Brs.) × Oncidium (Onc.) × Odontoglossum (Odm.) × Miltonia (Milt.)

Bloom Season: Spring, Summer, Autumn

Degarmoara Admiralty Island 'Radiant' × Odcdm. Camano Island 'Goodale Moir'	Spotted brown to rich mahogany over gold to lavender background
Mtssa. Citron × Odcdm. Costa Rica 'Vashon'	Gold to yellow flowers with amber to chocolate markings
Bak. Roy Seger	Sunset hues
Mtssa. Mossy Knoll 'Persian Tapestry' × Odcdm. Costa Rica 'Vashon'	Chocolate flowers with yellowish lips
Brsdm. Klara Ahrnke 'Vashon' × Oda. Debutante × Odm. Yukon Harbor 'Tall Warrior'	Brown and yellow flowers

Beallara (Bllra.)—Miltonia (Milt.) × Brassia (Brs.) × Odontoglossum (Odm.) × Cochlioda (Cda.)

Bloom Season: Spring, Summer, Autumn

Mtssa. Mossy Knoll 'Arabian Legend' × Red Knight 'Dark Brilliance'	Dark mahogany and/or chocolate spots; dark black chocolate flowers
Bllra. Tahoma Glacier 'Sugar Sweet' AM/AOS	Cream base with burgundy spots on sepals and petals; white lip, burgundy spots, gold crest
Bllra. Tahoma Glacier 'Z-8' × O. Golden Glacier 'Sunshine'	Large yellow flowers; some spots

Bllra. Tahoma Glacier 'The Minx' × Odm. Golden Ransom 'Pride of Vashon'	Yellow to whitish flowers; darker spotting on segments
Bllra. 'Lavender Leopard'	Small yellow flowers heavily suffised with brown dots

Burrageara (Burr.)—Miltonia (Milt.) × Oncidium (Onc.) × Odontoglossum (Odm.) × Cochlioda (Cda.)

Bloom Season: Variable (twice a year)

Mtdm. Millicent Brown × Oda Red Knight	Chocolate colors with gold markings

Colmanara (Colm.)—Odontoglossum (Odm.) × Miltonia (Milt.) × Oncidium (Onc.)

Bloom Season: Variable

Colm. Cauca Valley 'Golden Surprise' × Odm. Yukon Harbor 'Giant'	Brown, gold, and yellow flowers

Degarmoara (Dgmra.)—Miltonia (Milt.) × Brassia (Brs.) × Odontolgossum (Odm.)

Bloom Season: Variable

Mtssa. Green Goddess × Odm. Pachecoe 'Vashon' AM/AOS	Yellow and gold overlaid with dark brown
Brs. verrucosa × Odtna. Glass Creek 'Raspberry Sundae'	Yellow with chocolate-black spots
Mtssa. Citron × Odm. hallii	Yellow to lemon tones marked with brown spots

Mtssa. Citron 3100 × Odm. Yukon Harbor 'Summer Gold'	Brownish yellow sepal and petal with amber spots
Mtssa. Mossy Knoll 'May' × Odm. Yukon Harbor 'Summer Gold'	Flowers rich red, brown, gold with brown and amber markings
Dgmra. Orcus Island 'Vashon' HCC/AOS × Onc. Gold Coin Butte 'Hercules'	Large lavender-toned flowers; dark spotting on lip
Mtssa. Citron × Odm. Yukon Harbor	Yellow flowers

Forgetara (Fgtra.)—Miltassia (Mtssa.) × Aspasia (Asp.)

Bloom Season: Variable

Mtssa. Aztec × *Asp. principissa*	Tan sepals and petals; white lip
Mtssa. Erachne × Milt. Lanikai × *Asp. principissa*	Bronze to lavender blooms; white to pastel mauve lip

Maclellanara (McLna.)—Brassia (Brs.) × Oncidium (Onc.) × Odontoglossum (Odm.)

Bloom Season: Variable

Brsdm. Klara Ahrnke × Odm. Yukon Harbor	Yellow and gold flowers with darker chocolate markings
Mclna. Pagan Lovesong 'Everglades' AM/AOS	Pale chartreuse sepals; petals blotched with chocolate

Vuylstekeara (Vuyl.)—Cochlioda (Cda.) × Miltonia (Milt.) × Odontoglossum (Odm.)

Bloom Season: Winter, Spring

Vuyl. Cambria 'Plush' FCC/ RHS/AOS	Red and white flowers, outstanding
Vuyl. Cambria 'Lensings Favorite'	Mottled red flowers, pink flush petals
Vuyl. 'Edna Stamperland'	Small red-orange flowers; excellent

Wilsonara (Wils.)—Odontoglossum (Odm.) × Oncidium (Onc.) × Cochlioda (Cda.)

Bloom Season: Variable

Oda. vuylstekeara × *Onc. schilleranum*	Delicate brown flowers, from amber to lighter buff
Onc. Honolulu × Oda. Alliance	Chocolate tones with gold tips on the segments
Wils. Golden Tiger	Lovely brown and gold stripes
Wils. Acemanda 'Everglades' SM/SFOS	Fire engine red and white flowers
Oda. Memoria Helen Scholle 'Lilac Time' × Onc. Gold Coin Butte 'Taxco'	Chocolate brown with some yellow on petal tips; yellow lip speckled with chocolate color
Odcdm. Unimak Island 'Golden Abundance' × Red Knight 'Velvet Cloak'	Calico flowers and reddish brown to cinnamon brown with yellow markings; yellow lip

Odcdm. Tiger Butter 'Pride of Vashon' AM/AOS × Oda. Olympic Flame 'Pride of Vashon' AM/AOS	Dark yellow and gold flowers with brown markings
Five Oaks 'Golden Leaf' AM/ AOS	Large yellow with brown markings, white lip

15

Paphiopedilum

(*paff*-ee-oh-*ped*-ill-um)

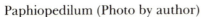

Paphiopedilums, the lady slippers, offer the home grower a galaxy of colorful flowers in breathtaking color, shapes, and sizes. Extensive hybridization has resulted in an enormous number of varieties, and individual growers have their own special ones. Originally bred from seventy known species, literally thousands of hybrids are now available, and most are ideal houseplants that require little care.

Paphiopedilum (Photo by author)

These multicolored orchids are usually terrestrial, but few growers use soil for them; the standard potting mix is fine-grade fir bark with some peat or perlite or some pieces of Styrofoam or charcoal chips. The plants are from intermediate or tropical climates, from the Far East, the ranges of the Himalayas, through Southeast Asia, Borneo, and New Guinea. A number of species also grow in the Philippines, and perhaps the greatest number of Paphiopedilums come from Borneo and Thailand.

Bearing attractive plain green or mottled foliage and without pseudobulbs, the plants produce large 4-inch flowers on single scapes, generally in winter to spring. The mottled-leaved types such as *Paph. bellatulum* and *Paph. niveum* require somewhat warm temperatures; plain-leaved types such as *Paph. praestans* and *Paph. sanderianum* like somewhat cool temperatures. Somewhere in between is a large group of species that has either mottled or plain green leaves and is best grown with Cattleya conditions; these plants include *Paph. barbatum, Paph. callosum, Paph. fairieanum,* and *Paph. insigne* (probably the most popular because it is so easy to grow and has exquisite apple-green striped flowers).

Paphiopedilum flowers, which have a somewhat waxy texture and a sac lip, are very long-lasting, up to six weeks. People in my shop often ask if the plants are insect eaters. They are not. The sac is simply the device used to ensnare and capture insects for pollination purposes.

Paphiopedilums are generally low-light subjects and can bloom even at a north window. It is this amazing facility that makes them so desirable indoors where light is none too good. In their native environment, Paphiopedilums grow on the floor of the jungle, where large canopies of tree branches keep them in almost continuous shade. Thus diffused light is a necessity. Avoid sunlight because direct rays—even in the home where sun is subdued—can scorch foliage.

Experiment with Paphiopedilums in your home. Sometimes a move of a few inches one way or another can make the difference between a plant that really grows and one that just exists. Once plants find their place in the home and are growing well, do not move them about.

Some orchids are not successful under artificial lamps, but Paphiopedilums do brilliantly there. All in all, they are excellent plants for the beginning hobbyist; they are relatively inexpensive and offer great rewards. A dozen plants provide color for months.

Growing Conditions

Lady slipper orchids can tolerate a wide range of temperatures, but 58° to 60°F at night is ideal for most varieties, with higher temperatures during the day. (Mottled-leaved types need slightly warmer nighttime temperatures, about 62°F.) However, all Paphiopedilums require a good circulation of air, so do avoid a stagnant atmosphere.

Good humidity, a necessity for many orchids, is not imperative with most Paphiopedilums, and plants adjust to 20% humidity. In fact, excessive humidity can cause trouble, especially in winter when days tend to be cloudy.

Watering and Feeding

Paphiopedilums need year-round, evenly moist compost that drains readily. Do not grow them too dry; none can withstand a dry compost.

If possible, use tepid water (that has stood overnight) for lady slippers. Icy water can shock roots. Water copiously during summer and fall; reduce watering somewht in spring after most plants bloom, but again, do not let the compost become dry.

Avoid excessive misting and high humidity. Do not let water stand in the leaf axils; that can cause rot. When you water, do it thoroughly; scanty watering creates dry pockets and forces roots to search for moisture, weakening the plant. Occasionally, about once every six weeks, leach out toxic salts by immersing the plants to the rim of the pot in a sinkful of water for a few hours.

The Paphiopedilums require moderate feeding; a general plant food of 20-10-10 is fine twice a month.

Potting Mixes and Repotting

Years ago I used equal parts soil and fir bark for Paphiopedilums, but I found that the compost at times became waterlogged and growth was inhibited. I now use a fine-grade bark mix and add a little perlite and a few charcoal chips. Lava-rock pellets are a good addition, too. The ideal compost drains readily and dries quickly. Plants need good drainage to prosper.

Repot your plants every year; lady slippers do not like being potbound and benefit from larger pots each year. When repotting, be sure you remove dead roots and all old compost; the roots should be quite clean before repotting. The plants generally like tight potting; that is, they must be firm and not wobble in the pot. To repot a Paphiopedilum, grasp the plant at the crown; hold the crown firmly in one hand and tease the plant out of the old compost. Never pull at it or you might harm the roots.

After repotting, water well. Thoroughly moisten the new bark, and do not water for about three to five days. Then water scantily for a few weeks until you see new tips of roots searching for water; now start a regular watering schedule.

Golden Brown Hybrids

Bloom Season: Autumn, Winter

Sheila Hanes × Golden Acres 'Golden Green' AM/AOS

Liz Greenlees 'Betty's Sister' × Golden Acres 'Royal Green' AM/AOS

Yerba Buena 'Whitecap' HCC/AOS × Lillianne 'Rosy Too' BM/CSA

Yellow Hybrids

Bloom Season: Autumn, Winter

Sheila Hanes × Bantry Bay

Divisadero 'Val' HCC/AOS × Bantry Bay

Liz Greenlees 'Betty's Sister' × Bantry Bay

Hellas F2 × 'Sunrise'

Red–Burgundy Hybrids

Bloom Season: Autumn, Winter, Spring

Redvale 'Sunspot' × Futura 'Silver Lining'

Red Beauty 'Lava Flow' × Wendarrow 'Storm'

Carl Keyes 'Bion' × Valwin

Jim Iverson 'All Red' × Valwin 'Bion' HCC/AOS

Tommie's Delight 'Rose Red' × Dezred 'Universe'

Carlwin 'Wizard' × Winsheba 'Sprite'

Outrigger '4975' × Vallantis 'Rex'

Vallarrow 'Red Rock' HCC/AOS × Red Robin 'Select'

Headlands Marblehead 'Julius' × Winlantis 'Quirinus' BM/CSA

Rewa Symons 'Victorian Rose' × Cheryl Ann Boyd 'Charm'

Bunker Hill 'Red Coat' × Rewa Symons 'Victorian Rose'

Smooth '93071' × Sioux

Sioux 'Amethyst' × Amanda 'Joyance' AM/RHS

Omdurman 'Oases' HCC/AOS × Vallantis 'Rex J.'

Farnmoore 'Rex'

Orchilla 'Chilton' × Wendarrow

Pueblo 'Animas'

Jim Iverson × Valwin Mt. Madonna

Paeony 'Regency' × Carl Keyes 'Bion'

Mahogany Hybrids

Bloom Season: Autumn, Winter, Spring

Cavalli-Sforza Amber Star 'Chilton' × Winston Churchill 'Redoubtable' FCC/AOS

Winlantis 'Tectona' × Yeat's Country 'Open Spaces'

Cheryl Ann Boyd 'Darjeeling' × Yeat's Country 'Open Spaces'

Omdurman 'Morocco' × Florence Wilks 'Supreme'

Portovan 'Princely' × Florence Wilks 'Supreme'

Everett Wilcox 'Red Chief' HCC/AOS × Vallarrow 'Red Challenge' HCC/AOS

Pittsburg 'Banner' × Yeat's Country 'Open Spaces'

Old Cedar 'Polished' × Milrow 'Old Pecan'

Milionette 'Red Flame' × Everett Wilcox 'Hastings' HCC/AOS

Green and Green-Yellow Hybrids
Bloom Season: Winter, Spring

Chief Eagle Hellas 'Westonbirt' FCC/AOX × Burleigh Mohur

Sheila Hanes 'Shamrock' × Shapely 'Geisha'

Meadow Mist 'Tricolor' × Fall Tones 'Golden Rod'

Greenvale 'Christine' × Jolly Green Gem 'Hercules'

Via Jardin Lustroso 'Wrights' × Van Ness 'Sprite'

Merce-Lou Audino

Wallur 'Lemon' × Lambert Day 'Sweet Lime'

Stan Bachman's Choice × LaCrescent 'Moonglow'

Oasis 'Outlook' × LaCrescent 'Moonglow'

Le Hocq Point 'Sea Mist' × Supreme Court × Minster Lovell

Ronez Point 'Pippin' × Prime Time 'Clear Day'

Yerba Buena 'White Cap' HCC/AOS × Overlay 'Saffron'

Divisidero 'Val' × Van Ness

Bell o' Ireland

Shapely 'Geisha' × Dalla 'Viking'

Prime Time 'Breath of Spring' × La Honda × Malibu

Prime Time 'Clear Day' × Silver Dollar 'Amulet'

Diversion 'Green Glory' × Prime Time 'Clear Day'

Yerba Mate 'Iceberg' × Overlay 'Green Gold'

Denehurst 'Surprise' × Little Irene 'Winter Blessing'

Mystic Jewel (provisional) (Alma Gavaert 'Mme. Mertens' × Makuli 'Springtime')

Makuli (Makuli 'Meadowsweet' × Makuli 'Emerald' HCC/AOS)

Makuli (Makuli 'Adventurine' HCC/AOS × Makuli 'Emerald' HCC/AOS)

Oriental Frieze (provisional) (Gowerianum 'Green Ghost' × Makuli 'Seaform')

Insigne sanderae × Makuli 'Emerald' HCC/AOS

Hybrids with Beautiful Variegated Foliage

Bloom Season: Autumn, Winter

Alma Gavaert 'Madam Mertens'

Clair de Lune var. Edgar Von Belle AM/AOS

Maudiae 'Magnificum'

Hybrids Spotted White or Brushed Colored Dorsal

Bloom Season: Winter, Spring

World Exploit 'Jet Set' × Diversion 'New Orleans' AM/AOS

Jim Dandy 'Regent' × Valwin 'Triumph'

Hunston 'Woodlands' × Beauté '11164'

Ace High 'Rotunda' × Indian Ocean 'Giant'

Mahaska '347' × Happy Tweed '3147'

Cavalese 'Giganteum' × Pacific Glen 'Stately'

Spotted Hybrids

Bloom Season: Winter, Spring

Holywell

Boston Tea Party '1164' × Winston Churchill 'Indomitable' FCC/AOS

Flight Path 'Tree Village' × Winston Churchill 'Redoubtable' FCC/AOS

Marlborough

Tree of Reminiscence

Tree of Goshima 'Tree Village' × Winston Churchill 'Redoubtable' FCC/AOS

Tree of Reminiscence

Motoo Kimura

Compton 'Chilton' × Winston Churchill 'Redoubtable' FCC/AOS

Hiroko Kimura

Claret Tree

Paph. Via Sonrisa

Normandy × Pacific Ocean 'Anne' AM/AOS

Rose Flash × Gitana 'Joe'

Species

Bloom Season: Variable.

Paph. barbatum has tessellated foliage and white, green, and purple flowers.

Paph. bellatulum has a dwarf habit and is summer-blooming. Creamy white flowers are about 2 inches across. Sepals and petals are heavily spotted and marked with maroon.

Paph. callosum has impressive 3- to 4-inch flowers borne on 12- to 15-inch stems; foliage is mottled green. Blooms in spring-summer.

Paph. concolor has a dwarf habit and is summer-blooming. Flowers are about 2 inches across and are light yellow speckled with minute red dots. Foliage is mottled.

Paph. godefroyae produces creamy yellow or white spotted and blotched brown-purple flowers in the summer.

Paph. hirsutissimum, spring-blooming, has flowers about 6 inches across.

Paph. insigne has green leaves and large flowers; colors vary greatly.

Paph. niveum has a dwarf habit and is summer-blooming. Flowers are about 2 inches across, satiny white with purple dots clustered toward the center.

Paph. niveum var. Ang. Thong is satin white with petals dotted mahogany. This summer bloomer may be a natural hybrid of *Paph. niveum* with either *Paph. bellatulum* or *Paph. godefroyae. P. niveum* 'Snow Dove' is a fine hybrid form, almost pure white.

Paph. parishii has bright, glossy green foliage; 5-inch petals are dark purple with green. The plant blooms in the summer.

Paph. philippinese, a summer and fall bloomer, has white sepals striped in reddish brown and green with contrasting yellow pouch.

Paph. praestans has large creamy white flowers, veined brown twisted petals.

Paph. sanderianum produces dark green leaves and remarkable large flowers; upper sepals pale yellow shaded green, petals ribbon-like with purple-brown spots.

Paph. sukhakulii is a combination of green, white, and maroon. The sac is brown to maroon. The orchid blooms at various times.

16

Phalaenopsis

(*fail*-ee-en-*op*-sis)

Certainly no other orchid has attained the popularity of the Phalaenopsis. These plants with dark green spatula-shaped leaves and graceful wands of flowers that last for months are a sheer delight. Plants also produce successive blooms; after they fade, cut above a node to induce another cycle of bloom. Coming from the Far East—many from Assam and Burma, and a great quantity from the Philippines—Phalaenopsis are sometimes called moon flowers because the blossoms last longer than a full moon. Their most common name is moth orchid, not because the flowers really resemble moths but because the name *phalaina* means moth. They are also sometimes called the dogwood orchid because the white varieties resemble the common dogwood tree flowers.

In the wild, the plants are epiphytic or lithophytic and almost always grow in areas of shade. Without pseudobulbs like most orchids, Phalaenopsis need a humid atmosphere. Hybridization has produced some that can tolerate less than a saturated condition, but the majority still like 50% humidity. They will flourish in the home with less humidity, but eventually—in about two years—the plants will need adequate humidity. It is not difficult to furnish some additional humidity in the home, as discussed in Chapter 4.

The Phalaenopsis genus has been hybridized almost as extensively as the plants in the Cattleya tribe. There are virtually thousands of hybrids; once, only twenty years ago, we saw only white moth orchids, but today flowers come in a remarkable array of colors, from yellow to pink to lavender. Many varieties even have candy-striped flowers.

Because of their ability to withstand low light—and indeed flourish in it—the Phalaenopsis have become popular houseplants. And although a Cattleya is impressive in the home for decoration, very few flowers can beat the graceful elegance of the Phalaenopsis in full

Phalaenopsis (Photo by author)

bloom. They are a sight to behold and make any ordinary setting beautiful.

The most famous Phalaenopsis is *Phal. amabilis;* with its many varieties, it is the cornerstone of most modern white hybrids today. From this heritage came Phal. Doris and subsequent hybrids such as the world-famous Phal. Grace Palm, a large, well-formed, extremely beautiful white. Recently, *Phal. amboinensis,* from an island near New Guinea, a pale yellow species with markings, has been used in hybridization with outstanding results.

Growing Conditions

For many years, I grew Phalaenopses in warm temperatures—to 80°F during the day and about 65°F at night. However, I have found that lowering the night temperature in October to, say, 60°F or a few degrees lower sometimes produces more bloom. Some area in your home is certain to be cooler than others, and this is the place to put your plants in the late fall to encourage flowering. Coolness seems to produce more branching as well, in most varieties.

Like most orchids, Phalaenopsis like a buoyant atmosphere; in a stagnant situation they will do little growing. Mature specimens of the larger plants can tolerate somewhat low humidity (20% to 30%) without harm, but most Phalaenopsis like an area of good air circulation. This air should not be cold, however; a steady flow of warm air is ideal. Keep fans running most of the time.

Phalaenopsis like a somewhat shady but not dark area; the light should be diffused. For example, the patterned window glass found in many bathrooms provides almost ideal light for Phalaenopsis. (Perhaps this accounts for so many flourishing Phalaenopsis in bathrooms.)

Direct sun in winter is suitable for plants but not mandatory. If your orchids are at a west or south window, be sure there is a screen or movable blind to protect the plants from direct sun. In summer, putting moth orchids in direct sun is fatal to the plants; you must provide some protection from the strong rays.

I cannot stress too much that Phalaenopsis are highly susceptible to leaf scorch from direct sun, so be guided accordingly. These are ideal plants for a somewhat bright place in the home.

Watering and Feeding

With Phalaenopsis the proper watering schedule is vital. These plants have no pseudobulbs to store nutrients or water, yet overwatering can be dangerous. With too much moisture, the compost becomes soggy, plant roots suffocate, and the plant succumbs.

Although the natural habitat of Phalaenopsis may seem to dictate a saturated environment, in cultivation the plants react somewhat differently. The best way to water Phalaenopsis is to keep an evenly moist compost—never dry, never soggy. This is not easy and requires some experimentation and patience on your part.

Plants in small pots will need more water than those in large containers because small pots dry out quickly. Varieties in clay pots will need more water than those in plastic pots because plastic holds moisture longer. Water large pots (7 inches and over) twice a week in spring and summer, once a week the rest of the year. Water small pots (to 6 inches) every other day in warm weather, every fifth day the rest of the year unless the weather is unusually cloudy and cool; then water only once every seven to ten days. In all cases, if you are undecided about watering, underwater.

How you water Phalaenopsis makes a difference, too. Phalaenopsis are particularly vulnerable to water accumulating in the crown of the plant. This can cause rot, so hand water your plants.

The moth orchids must also have a well-devised feeding program. Use Peters general orchid food (30-10-10) three or four times a month in warm weather and about twice a month the rest of the year. Apply a supplemental feeding of Atlas Fish Emulsion during the greatest time of growth, usually in summer.

Potting Mixes and Repotting

Phalaenopsis will grow in fir bark, crushed rock, charcoal, and even broken bricks with about the same results: plants flourish. Generally, the potting mix is not important for Phalaenopsis as long as the material drains readily. I successfully use medium-grade fir bark for my Phalaenopsis, mixed with a few charcoal chips.

Repot plants only when the medium has deteriorated—when it is pulverized and brownish black—generally in about eighteen months. The exception is seedlings, which do have to be shifted to larger pots as growth progresses. Seedlings should be repotted at least two or three times before they reach their fourth year, at which time they can grow under the same conditions as a mature specimen.

Repotting these orchids is not easy, because roots clamber over and attach themselves to almost any surface, so removing the roots is a delicate task. Some breakage is virtually impossible to prevent. Many times I break the old pot if it is clay and try to avoid injuring plant roots by pulling them loose from surfaces.

Once you have the plant out of the container, remove all old compost and trim away dead brown roots; center the plant in a pot with shards and fill in and around with bark. Pot somewhat tightly for best results. After potting, water thoroughly and let the plant stay without water a few days. Then resume the normal watering schedule.

White Phalaenopsis

The large white Phalaenopsis are perhaps the most popular orchids. Generally, they are not difficult to care for, and their long-lasting flowers make even a nongardener appear to be a good one. Their place in the home as a decorative accent is well established, and in the category of white we find a realm of beauty unsurpassed by most flowers. They are superb.

There has been intense hybridization within the white color arena.

Plants like Phal. Winter Maiden and Phal. Winter Beauty 'York' AM/ AOS exhibit beautifully formed large flowers (to 5 inches) with dozens to a scape. Many whites have contrasting colored lips to further their beauty, Phal. Prairie Du Sac × Phal. Mauston being a prime example.

Recently, hybrid whites have appeared that offer branching spikes with as many as one hundred flowers to a plant. This additional heritage from *Phal. schillerana* or *Phal. stuartiana* has greatly increased the popularity of Phalaenopsis. Specimen plants in 12-inch pots look like Phalaenopsis trees, some scaling to 4 feet with multiple branching habit.

The Hausermann Orchid Company of Villa Park, Illinois, has extensively bred Phalaenopsis and offers an array of plants to dazzle the eye. Its catalog lists hundreds of hybrids in all areas: pink, yellow, candy stripe, and so forth.

White Phalaenopsis hybrids are easy to grow in average home temperatures of 58°F at night, but they do require good air circulation. Diffused light suits the plants, and even moisture at the roots is the ideal situation; most plants do not need a drying-out period. Feed your Phalaenopsis on a regular basis using Peters 30-10-10 plant food most of the year, but in summer switch to Peters 10-30-20.

These are excellent plants for beginners as well as more experienced growers. Within the white hybrids there is something for every eye.

White Phalaenopsis Hybrids

Bloom Season: Winter, Spring

Winter Maiden × Lafayette

Carl Hausermann × Winter Maiden AM/AOS

Winter Beauty 'York' AM/AOS

Barbara Lynn × Prairie Du Chien

Prairie Du Chien × Winter Beauty AM/AOS

Winter Maiden

Ice Sculpture

Cherryvale '#1' × Evangeline 'Exquisita'

Cherryvale

Portola 'Mt. Madonna' × Muriel Turner 'Corcoran'

Portola 'Mt. Madonna' × Grace Palm '51'

Portola 'Mt. Madonna' × Norman Peterson × Polar Gull '#1'

White with Red Lip Phalaenopsis Hybrids

Bloom Season: Winter, Spring

Prairie Du Sac × Mauston

Prairie Du Sac × self

Cher Ann 'York' HCC/AOS × Mauston

Pink, Lavender, and Purple Phalaenopsis

In the last decade great strides have been made in breeding pink—and shades of pink—Phalaenopsis. There are plants with pale pink flowers, those with flowers in a deep rose color and many shades between. Plants carry somewhat medium-sized flowers—smaller than those in the white categories—but most varieties have many, many blooms. Phal. Dorisellita × Hokuspokus × Phal. Monticello is a prime example of an exquisite pink Phalaenopsis. More so than whites, some pinks have a branching habit contributed by Doritis lineage, but sometimes this can be a disadvantage rather than an advantage. The wildly branching types lose something in elegance and beauty, and the designs of the branching, to the left, right, here and there, creates a busy pattern that can assault the eye.

In general, the plants are robust with thick stems and grow well in an intermediate situation with routine Phalaenopsis care, as previously described. There are no special tricks, and bloom season is variable, although most pinks are at their bloom peak in early spring.

Pink Phalaenopsis Hybrids

Bloom Season: Autumn, Winter, Spring

Uvaldo × Beard's Sunshine

Hokuspokus × Beard's Sunshine

Zauberrose × Lippstadt × Monticello

Dorisellita × Hokuspokus × Monticello

Arlene Andrews

But Beautiful '#3' × Rose Girl '#1'

Sweet Dreams 'A3' × Zauberrot 'Largo'

Zauberrose '#1' × Diana '#1'

Zada's Best '#1 Pink Lip' × Zauberrose '#2 Dark'

Yellow Phalaenopsis

In the last few years the yellow Phalaenopsis, once a hybridist's dream, has become a reality. Yellow is always a desirable color, and in the Phalaenopsis genus it works very well indeed. There is a wide range of yellows; some varieties are pale yellow, others, such as Hausermann's Phal. Gold Cup 'Everlasting,' are almost true yellow. Many have faint markings: red barring, brown dotting, and so forth.

The yellow Phalaenopsis do not branch as much as the pinks, and stems are not usually as stout as in the white or pink categories. Flowers may be small, to about 2 inches across, or larger, to about 5 inches. Some varieties, such as Phal. Paul Hausermann 'Yellow Ribbon' AM/AOS, have a contrasting color lip, making the plants very appealing, and I think we will see more of these crosses in the coming years. The hybridists seem to be following the same trail as they did with the whites.

Generally, the yellows are not as easy to grow as other Phalaenopsis. Too much moisture affects them adversely, and these plants are not as strong as other hybrids. Lately, I have been resting the yellows slightly after they flower—about a month or so—with less water than usual. Bloom season is variable but usually at its peak in spring.

I would not yet recommend these plants for the beginner, as beautiful as they are. In a few years I believe we will see stronger and more compliant plants to grow.

Yellow Phalaenopsis Hybrids

Bloom Season: Spring

Phal. Kewaunee × *Phal. amboinensis*

Sun Prairie 'Yellow Star'

Hausermann's Elegance × Wyocena

Paula Hausermann 'Sunshine' HCC/AOS

Shellie Lynn × Barbara Moler

Golden Buddha × Hausermann's Elegance

Desert Wind

Gold Cup 'Everlasting'

Tyler Carlson '#1' × Sands Whim '#1'

Paul Hausermann 'Yellow Ribbon' AM/AOS

Brandenburg '#1' × Golden Amboin '#2'

Golden Amboin

Brandenburg '#1' × Tyler's Travels 'Santa Cruz'

Red Phalaenopsis

The elusive red flower is always an objective for growers. And just as growers have succeeded with Cattleyas (after many years of hybridizing), they are now coming close to opening the frontier of red Phalaenopsis. The most promising parent for this coalition is *Phal. violacea,* and the results so far have been encouraging. The colors are not as bright as one would want, but I believe that in time this hurdle will be surmounted.

The red Phalaenopsis I have seen are somewhat smaller plants than, say, their white hybrid cousins, but flowers are of heavy substance and fairly large—to about 2 inches across. Plants grow with the same conditions as those for the novelty or striped varieties.

Red Phalaenopsis Hybrids

Bloom Season: Autumn, Winter

Phal. Winter Dawn × Phal. Luedde-Violacea × *Phal. fasciata* × *Phal. amboinensis*

Phal. Luedde-Violacea × *Phal. fasciata* 'Cherryvale' × Phal. Princess Kaiulani 'Carriage Hill' AM/AOS

Coral Isles 'York' AM/AOS × Golden Buddha 'Carriage Hill'

Carnival 'Bonsall' HCC/AOS × Golden Buddha 'Carriage Hill'

Princess Lorraine 'Flaming Star' HCC/AOS × Freed's Danseuse 'Treva' HCC/AOS

Phal. Coral Isles × *Phal. lueddemanniana* × Phal. Violet Charm

Dorisellita 'Midnight' HCC/AOS × Allspice 'Ft. Worth'

George Vasquez 'Flaming Glory' HCC/AOS × Freed's Danseuse 'Treva' HCC/AOS

Phal. gigantea × *Phal. mariae* × Phal. Malibu Imp 'Rieta' AM/AOS

Sophie Hausermann × Vitrail 'Bon Bon'

Red Wine 'Ruby' × George Vasquez 'Flaming Glory' HCC/AOS

Penang 'York' AM/AOS × Coral Isle 'York' AM/AOS

Diane Rigg 'Lista' × Spica 'Florence' AM/AOS

Striped and Novelty Phalaenopsis

In this group are the breathtaking candy-stripe hybrids, the exquisite spotted varieties such as Phal. Carnival 'Bonsall' AM/AOS, and an odd assortment of what I call novelty colors—peach, copper with or without spots, and muted pastel shades blotched or reticulated. There are hundreds; Robert Wescott's catalog featuring the Herb Hager collection lists some three hundred different art or novelty shades.

I have found the novelty Phalaenopsis quite appealing, and they grow with but little care. Furthermore, most of them bloom when only three years old, and many, many varieties are inexpensive. Plants tolerate a range of temperatures (56°F at night) without harm. This is an excellent category for beginners. You almost cannot go wrong even if you are a clumsy gardener.

Striped and Novelty Phalaenopsis Hybrids

Bloom Season: Winter, Spring

Painted Cave 'York' HCC/AOS	White with red spots
Class President 'Willowbrook'	Yellow with bright red markings
Winter Carnival × Jean Mc-Farlin	White with spots and stripes

Magdalene Acker × Wyocena	Peach-pink
Carnival 'Bonsall' × Welcome Home	White with lavender blotching
Gold Coin × Welcome Home	White with lavender spotting
Amy Hausermann × Kewaskum	White with stripes and dots
Donald Rigg 'Peaches' × Wyocena	Peach-copper tones
Cayanne	Rosy lavender to tannish brown
Seeing Double	White background with lavender-magenta spotting
Autumn Symphony	Yellow
Side Show	Magenta; spotted
Jim's Flame	Light cream to magenta pink; spotted
Redwine 'Burgundy' × *Phal. lueddemanniana* 'Pulchra #1'	Magenta
Star Bright 'Red' × Rose Girl '#2'	Lavender-reds
Samba's Girl	Light pink
Milstead 'Orinda' × Penny Candy 'Sunset'	Pastel lavender, orange, yellow
Shirley Gill 'Elsner' × Herb Hager 'Santa Cruz'	Medium to dark pink
Ambotrana 'Burgundy' × Diana '#1'	Lavender-magenta
Dear Barbara '#2' × Golden Duplicate 'Virg Ford'	Cream to yellow

Sweet Dreams '#5' × Zauber-rot 'Largo'	Lavender-pink
Golden Amboin '#1' × Star of Florida 'Ambo'	Yellow through mahogany
Golden Grant '#1' × Penang 'Lovely' HCC/AOS	Yellow
Penang	Cream-yellow
Sweet Dreams	Cream-white; spotted
Princess Samba 'Corcoran' HCC/AOS × Psilantha 'Ford'	Yellow
Samba 'Saber Dance' HCC/AOS × Brazilian Glow 'Corcoran' AM/AOS	Cream-white

Miniature Multiflora Phalaenopsis

Bloom Season: Variable

Good Cheer 'Cutie' × *Phal. schillerana* 'Purpurea #1'

Good Cheer 'Cutie' × Giggles 'A'

Adeline Anderson 'Mimi' × *Phal. schillerana* 'Jungle Light'

Be Glad 'Santa Cruz' × Melinda Nan 'Jones'

Be Glad

Cassandra 'Santa Cruz' × Larry Oberhaus '#1'

Be Glad '#1' × Pink Minuet 'Dark'

Little Kris 'Bright Future' × Malibu Frolic 'Pink Show'

Memoria Lil Schrager 'Classic' × Be Glad 'Louisa'

Doritaenopsis—Doritis × Phalaenopsis

Doritaenopsis is a cross of Doritis and Phalaenopsis. This separate genus's offspring are generally darker colored than Phalaenopsis. Flowers are somewhat smaller than the typical Phalaenopsis blooms, but there are many to a scape, and the colors—dark lavenders, fuschias—have almost a phosphorescent hue; they literally glow. Most Doritaenopsis hybrids bear vertical stems in a very handsome candelabrum effect. The lasting quality of the flowers is amazing: plants stay in bloom for over six months!

Most varieties can tolerate coolness at night; 55°F does not harm them. Shade plants from strong summer sun. These are fine subjects for the home, making a bold statement in any room.

Doritaenopsis Hybrids

Bloom Season: Winter, Spring

Junior Miss '#4' × Festivity 'Cutie'

Coral Gleam 'Samuel B. Mosher' FCC/AOS × *Phal. sumatrana* 'Red Knight' AM/AOS

Gorgeous Gold 'Canary' × Star of Florida 'Princess'

Dainty Miss 'Pink Miss' × Melanie Beard 'Bright Center'

Winneconne × Phal. Alfonso Ibarra

Pretty Nice 'York' AM/AOS

Ravenswood

Dtps. pulcherima 'Alba' × *Dtps. pulcherima* 'Kodama Blue'

Dtps. pulcherima 'Kodama Blue' × self

Species

Bloom Season: Variable

Phal. amboinensis has yellow sepals and petals with narrow transverse bars of brown; the waxy 2-inch flowers bloom in spring and summer.

Phal. cornu-cervi has 2-inch yellowish green flowers that are barred and blotched with red-brown. The lip is whitish. This decorative and unusual orchid blooms in the summer.

Phal. fasciata's 2-inch flowers have creamy white to pale yellow sepals and petals with narrow, transverse striping in mahogany brown. The plant blooms in the summer.

Phal. hiroglyphica has 2- to 2½-inch creamy white to pale yellow flowers; the sepals and petals are transversely barred in pale lavender to maroon. The white lip is spotted in lilac. This plant is an autumn bloomer.

Phal. mannii has yellow sepals and petals with cinnamon-brown barring or blotching and a white lip marked with purple. The plant blooms in the spring.

Phal. mariae has flowers about 1½ inches across. Sepals and petals are white, flushed yellow, amethyst-purple at the base. The plant is a winter bloomer.

Phal. schillerana, with marbled foliage; has large rose-purple flowers in the winter. The lip is similarly colored and spotted red at the base.

Phal. stuartiana, with mottled foliage, has branched, many-flowered scapes of variable lengths. The upper sepals and petals are white, sometimes with minute spottings of purple at the base. This orchid blooms in the winter.

Phal. sumatrana has near white to pale lemon yellow 2-inch flowers in the spring and summer. Sepals and petals are transversely barred with cinnamon to brownish red.

Phal. violacea (Malayan type) has shiny bright green foliage. The summer flowers are 2 inches. The dorsal sepals and petals are white, shaded with green, bright violet-purple at their bases.

Phal. violacea (Borneo type) has cream-colored sepals and petals, with a deep shade of reddish-purple on the innermost half. This is a summer bloomer.

Best of the Phalaenopsis

Winter Carnival 'Carousel'	White with red blotches
Debbie Dramm 'Johnny'	Candy stripe
Paula Hausermann 'Yellow Sunset'	Yellow
Sun Prairie 'York' AM/AOS	Yellow
Hausermann's Fireball	Excellent red
Class President 'Addison Trail'	Yellow with rich red markings
Winter Beauty 'York' AM/AOS	Fine large white
Dorisellita 'Pink Delight'	Rich red-purple

17

Vanda and Ascocenda

(*van*-dah, ass-coh-*send*-ah)

Characterized by long aerial roots and tough succulent strap-leaved foliage, the Vandas offer a colorful array of handsome large flowers in abundance. There are also cylindrical-leaved (terete) Vandas, but these are best grown outdoors in suitable climates, so I will not discuss them here. Vandas, a genus of over eighty species, come from China, the northern part of Australia, New Guinea, and the Himalayas. At one time Vandas, because of their height (some can reach 8 feet) and their light requirements (very sunny), were grown indoors only if there was a place outdoors for them to summer.

Hybridists realized the treasure of the long-lasting Vanda flowers and started crossing the plants with Ascocentrum, a genus of small plants with smaller flowers that require less light and are compatible with Vandas. The results have been a colorful array of beautiful small Vandas called Ascocendas—some only 12 inches high, others to 30 inches. Recently I have seen Ascocendas that rivaled Vandas in height.

However, even the large Ascocendas do not require as much light as Vandas, and they do flower profusely. In many varieties of Ascocendas the flower size is as large as in some Vandas, and bloom sometimes occurs twice a year.

The history of Vandas in England during the orchid craze is not much to talk about. The plants rarely survived the hothouse conditions the English thought they needed. Only recently have growers begun to understand Vandas. Hybridists have created a whole new world of exquisitely blue flowers, and shades of strawberry or yellow blossoms are highly prized.

The standard Vanda grows to 6 feet, although under cultivation the average height is about 4 feet. Plants have long aerial roots, are highly epiphytic, and dislike being restricted in a pot. Vandas need bright light to bloom, and this has been the difficulty in making them popular houseplants. But because the plants bloom in winter and spring, they are highly desirable for their flowers, which last several weeks. Large plants can produce many spikes with dozens of large flowers, a stunning display. *Vanda sanderiana* and V. Southeast Beauty 'Nate Strachar,' with large white flowers tinged green are prime examples.

Because of their growth habit—scandent aerial roots—Vandas and Ascocendas, and I use the two names interchangeably here, are best grown in open baskets of some type. Avoid redwood baskets, however, because the sap that exudes from the wood can harm plants. Teak baskets or those made from twigs or small branches work fine. Some of the smaller Ascocendas will grow in slotted clay pots. I have been successfully growing many this way.

Vanda (Photo by author)

Ascocenda (Photo by author)

Growing Conditions

Although Vandas need heat—most books recommend 80°F during the day and 65°F at night—the newer hybrids grow well in cooler temperatures at night (58°F). The main consideration is a free flow of air. In a closed situation the plants simply do not do well, although they will not die.

Vandas need good light—even the hybrids must have a few hours of bright light, or bloom will be sparse. Plants will not die in a less-than-light area, but they will not produce flowers readily. The best light in the home is at the top of windows or in the greenhouse near the roof.

Watering and Feeding

With Vandas, throw away all the rule books about watering. These plants are greedy for moisture and in the summer months need water every day; they should also be fed heavily during this time. I alternate Peters general plant food 30-10-10 with Peters Blossom Booster, 10-30-20, and I also apply Atlas Fish Emulsion twice a month. I periodically mist in the summer—whenever I walk by plants. The plants love a saturated atmosphere. Roots are long and will naturally grasp any surface they touch. Some of my plants have completely covered their teak baskets with roots, and those in clay pots have produced long aerial roots outside the pots.

If you can, suspend Vandas from the ceiling. An arboreal position suits them, and a summer outdoors, where they can benefit from rain and free air circulation, produces healthy plants.

There is no sure way to determine when a Vanda needs water. The plants are grown in large chunks of bark or charcoal, and the material will be dry a few hours after watering, so it is a question of getting to know the plants' needs by watching the leaf growth. Foliage should be dark green, perky, and upright. If a great number of aerial roots keep growing out of the container, water more. This method has been fairly successful for me.

Mist plants frequently in hot weather but do *not* mist leaves; aim the spray at the pot and growing medium; Vandas produce flowers from spikes between leaf axils, and too much water accumulating in this area can cause bud rot.

Potting Mixes and Repotting

More than any other orchids, Vandas resent being repotted; it sets them back considerably. Repot only every three or four years. I grow my plants in large-grade fir bark in clay pots or teak baskets, but I have also seen Vandas growing well in charcoal or cracked bricks or even stones. The potting mix is merely any porous material to hold the plant in place rather than a medium to supply nutrients. Avoid plastic containers for Vandas; they simply hold moisture too long.

To repot a Vanda you will have to break the pot. The tugging and teasing method that often works with other plants severely injures Vanda roots, and repotting a plant with long aerial roots is hardly a joy. It is difficult to restrict all roots to a new container, and lately I have been potting the plants with several roots outside the pot, some inside. After repotting, let the plant rest a few days *without water,* then water scantily the first few weeks to help combat the repotting shock Vandas are so susceptible to.

Vandas thrive in small pots or containers. As mentioned, the traditional way of growing them is in small teakwood baskets (available at some suppliers). Otherwise the standard slotted 4- or 5-inch pot is fine. Do not try to cram roots into a container; let them hang loose and wander as they will for best results.

Pink and Strawberry Vanda Hybrids

Bloom Season: Spring, Summer

Deva × Gordon Dillon

Josephine van Brero × Pimsai

Josephine van Brero × Madame Rattana

Memoria Louise Fuchs (name pending)

Thonglor 'T. Orchids #20' × Madame Marcos 'T. Orchids #1'

Bhimayothin

Nellie Morley 'Red Berry' AM/AOS

Jennie Hashimoto 'Chaleo' × Renton Hutchinson 'Orchidglade' AM/AOS

Blue Vanda Hybrids

Bloom Season: Autumn, Winter

V. Gordon Dillon 'Sapphire'

V. Kasem's Delight 'Dk. Blue' × Keeree 'Chiengmai' AM/RHT

V. Madame Rattana 'Dk. Red' × V. caerulea 'Chiengmai' AM/RHT

V. Manuel Torres

V. Rothschildiana

V. Springtime × V. caerulea

V. Suwapee

V. Fuch's Delight

V. Sumon Sophonsiri

V. Charungraks × *V. caerulea*

V. Wirat's Delight

V. Onomea

V. Hilo Princess 'Alice' AM/AOS

V. Hilo Blue

M. Judy Miyamoto 'Blue Velvet' AM/AOS

Red Vanda Hybrids

Bloom Season: Autumn, Winter

V. Josephine van Brero × Linda 'Red'

V. Madame Rattana × Aurawan

Yellow Ascocenda Hybrids

Bloom Season: Variable

Ascda. Theptong × V. Piyaporn

Ascda. Pinas 'Coqui' AM/AOS × Yip Sum Wah 'Boynton' AM/AOS

Ascda. Borincana

Ascda. Pong 'Orchidglade' × *V. tessellata*

Ascda. Marion Perreira

Ascda. Sunkist 'Voo Doo' AM/AOS × Capricorn 'Rainbow' FCC/AOS, SM/SFOS

Ascda. Viroonchan Gold 'Robert'

Ascda. Salva Dela Pena

Ascda. Inthira

Ascda. Fuch Gold

Ascda. 'Sunburst'

Peach Ascocenda Hybrids

Bloom Season: Variable

Ascda. Phairot × V. Charungraks

V. Eisensander × Ascda. Bonanza 'Bella Tew' AM/AOS

Medasand × Madame Kenny

V. Teoline Rosieglow 'Miss Hawaii' × *Ascda. curvifolium* 'Dream City'

V. lamellata var. Boxallii × Ascda. Too Soon 'Orchidglade'
SM/7WOC

Orange Ascocenda Hybrids

Bloom Season: Variable

Ascda. Medasand × *Ascda. miniatum*

V. Charungraks × Ascda. Madame Kenny

Ascda. Thonglor 'T. Orchids #2' × *Ascda. curvifolium*

V. Thananchai 'Niramon' AM/OST-RHT × Ascda. Tropicana
'Hatsue Akamine' AM/AOS

V. Aurawan × Ascda. Madame Kenny

Ascda. Bonanza 'Bella Tew' AM/AOS-HOS

Ascda. Yip Sum Wah 'Thai Treasure'

Ascda. Chaiyot 'Orange Crush' (meristem)

Ascda. Peggy Foo

Ascda. Oxbos

Pink Ascocenda Hybrids

Bloom Season: Variable

V. Nam Phung × Ascda. Dew-un

Ascda. Lenachai × Kasem

Ascda. Fiftieth State Beauty 'Mayumi' AM/HOS

Ascda. Irene Van Aistyne (name pending)

Ascda. Marlene Hinton

Ascda. Elizabeth Kendall

Ascda. Diane Fuchs

Ascda. Bonanza

Ascda. Cholburi

Blue Ascocenda Hybrids

Bloom Season: Variable

Ascda. Lenachai × *V. caerulea*

Ascda. Bangkok Beauty

Ascda. Boonchoo Bonanza × V. Varavuth

Ascda. Jean Ward (name pending)

Ascda. David Parker

Species

Bloom Season: Variable

V. cristata is a small plant about 9 inches high with short scapes. It bears exquisite 2-inch flowers, sepals and petals yellowish green, lips streaked with red and white lines. On the plant the flowers last over two months.

V. parishii has leaves 6 to 9 inches long and produces several scented flowers. They are 2 inches across, yellowish green spotted with red-brown.

V. roxburghii is about 24 inches tall, bears fragrant 2-inch pale green flowers splotched with brown; the small lip is lined with white and has a violet-purple disc. This is an easy-to-grow Vanda.

V. sanderiana is often called the queen of the Vandas. Its large handsome flowers are 5 inches across, almost flat; the soft pink color is suffused with white, the lower petals yellow crossed with red veins. The lip is intricate, tawny yellow streaked with red, the front part marked with chocolate brown.

Most Commonly Asked Questions

It seems the flowers of my Cattleyas get smaller and smaller every year. What's wrong?

Under greenhouse conditions with optimum light, flowers are generally larger than, say, plants grown in the home with less than ideal light.

I have had a difficult time getting my Cymbidiums to bloom yearly. Can you help?

Cymbidiums are not the easiest of orchids to rebloom, and usually non-blooming is due to temperatures. Most Cymbidiums require cool night temperatures to initiate buds. This cooling period is generally in late fall when plants should be grown at 45° to 55°F at night for about six weeks.

Have you any general advice for getting my Cattleyas to bloom? Some do and others do not.

Half a loaf is better than none, but to expect 100% bloom on all plants is asking a great deal. Most Cattleyas bloom better if night temperatures are somewhat cool (about 58°F). The heritage of the plant, however, may determine the way it blooms, so you might check out parentage to see if cool-growing or warm-growing parents were used and then adjust temperatures accordingly.

Some of the buds on my orchid plants shrivel and drop. What am I doing wrong?

It depends on what type of orchid you are growing, but bud drop is usually caused by a sudden fluctuation in temperature; toxic salts in the potting medium can be another cause, and not enough humidity in the air still a further reason.

Some of the backbulbs on my Cattleyas turn brown and die. Am I doing something wrong?

I doubt it. It is common for old backbulbs to die off after several years.

Some of my Cattleyas send up sheaths, but there are no buds inside. What causes this?

Many Cattleyas initiate sheaths and then wait several months for buds to form. Have patience.

What are the rules for growing orchids under artificial light?

There are too many rules to list here, but basically under lights orchids need excellent air circulation, a difference in day and night temperatures, and, most important, the timed light sequence must be correct. Some orchids need thirteen hours under lights, others fourteen, and so on. Consult a good book on growing plants under artificial light.

I want to grow some orchids on my windowsill. Can you suggest some easy ones for me?

I think I would start with Phalaenopsis. These plants can tolerate somewhat low light if necessary. The Paphiopedilums are also good subjects for windowsill growing.

I have trouble blooming Oncidiums. Can you help me?

I will try. Most Oncidiums require excellent light, and the potting medium should never be too wet. Hybrid Oncidiums with Odontoglossum heritage need somewhat cool nights to bloom (55°F). I would have to know the exact varieties you grow to be of more help.

Is it true that gas from the fireplace could harm my plants?

I doubt it, as long as there is sufficient air circulation in the room. Of course having plants too close to a roaring flame is just not advisable because of the heat buildup.

The lower leaves on some of my Paphiopedilums fall off. What is wrong?

It could be many things, but basically too much sun or too much water can cause this problem. Grow Paphs in a somewhat shaded place with average home conditions of 58°F at night and about 78°F during the day. Keep potting mix moderately moist but never soggy, and do not feed too much.

Is it true that too much plant food can result in many leaves and few flowers on some orchids?

Yes, if the plant food has high nitrogen content. Use a general plant food such as 30-10-10 or 20-10-10 a few months of the year and then switch to 10-30-20 the balance of the year.

What is the best kind of water to use for my Cattleyas and Paphiopedilums?

Most orchids respond very well to rainwater, but it is impossible to run around capturing raindrops. Generally if you can drink the water from your tap, it is fine for plants. However, if a high content of chlorine is used in your local water supply, allow a bucket of water to stand overnight before watering your plants.

I am confused by the term art shade in Cattleyas. Just what does this mean?

Art shades are the pastel colors such as peach, apricot, rust, and color ranges in between, as opposed to white or lavender.

Can you explain the secret of getting Phalaenopsis to rebloom? My local florist said something about cutting spikes midway down after flowers fade on top.

The secret is not a secret at all. Cut the spikes above a growing node after the top flowers fade, and usually the plants will rebloom in a few months.

What causes leaf tips to die back on some orchids? Is this serious?

I doubt if it is serious, but leaf tip die-back could be caused by too much fertilizer. Leach out the plant every month or so; take it to the sink and allow water to run through it for a few minutes.

What do you prescribe for ridding plants of mealybugs?

I usually use alcohol on a Q-Tip (or cotton bud), but most growers spray with malathion—not something I recommend for home use. Old tobacco steeped in water for a few days applied with a Q-Tip to insects also kills them.

Mildew has attacked some of my orchids. What am I doing wrong?

If night temperatures are cool (in the 50s) and humidity too high, botrytis can result in plants. Keep air moving in the growing area (a small fan works fine) and try to maintain warmer night temperatures by a few degrees.

Some of the lower leaves of my Phalaenopsis orchids are turning limp. Can you help?

Stop watering the plants so much and reduce humidity in the air. This may solve the problem. Occasionally, however, lower leaves of mature Phalaenopsis do naturally fade and die back.

Can you give me some advice about Vandas? My plants just do not bloom regularly, and I have some Vandas that have not bloomed in years, but their leaves have not died.

Vandas really require very high light intensity to bloom regularly; most average homes lack this. I suggest you try some of the new Ascocenda hybrids. These fine plants bloom with somewhat less light and bloom twice a year in good conditions.

Is it a good idea to summer orchids outdoors? Some growers have suggested this to me.

I really don't think so; usually the outdoor summer vacation is too short to do them any real good, and the plants may have trouble readjusting to its normal environment; this can be detrimental. With the exception of Vandas, which need high light, I would suggest orchids stay indoors unless of course you are in a year-round suitable climate.

What is the best potting medium for orchids? I have read that fir bark is widely used but other sources recommend osmunda, tree fern fiber, and other mediums.

There is no perfect potting medium for orchids, and there are as many recipes for a good potting mix as there are for apple pie. Generally, fir bark is used, and most hobbyists report good growing of plants in this medium. I suggest adding some charcoal chunks and perlite to the fir bark.

Should I rest Cattleyas after I repot them or stick to normal watering?

I would give the plants a slight rest—a few days—before resuming normal watering and a rest of at least a few weeks before feeding.

Glossary

Aerial roots Roots growing outside the potting mix or hanging free in air.

Agar A medium derived from seaweed, used as the base for seed-sowing mixtures.

Anther The part of the stamen containing pollen.

Asexual Propagation by division and meristem.

Axil The upper angle between a stem or branch and a leaf.

Backbulb The older pseudobulbs behind the growing lead.

Bifoliate Having two leaves.

Bigeneric Involving two genera in the parentage of a plant.

Bisexual Two-sexed, the flowers possessing both stamens and pistils.

Botanical Refers to species not grown for cut flowers.

Bract A leaflike sheath near the base of the flower stem.

Bulb Plant structure for storage purposes, usually underground, includes corm, rhizome, and tuber.

Bulbous Having the shape and character of a bulb.

Calyx Outer circle of floral parts, usually green.

Cellular Composed of cells.

Chlorotic Excessive yellowing due to a breaking down of the chlorophyll.

Chromosome A structure within the cell nucleus that carries the genes.

Clone A sexually produced seed-grown individual and all subsequent asexual (vegetative) propagations.

Column	The central body of the orchid flower formed by the union of the stamens and pistil.
Community pot	The container used for many seedlings.
Compost	Decomposed vegetable matter.
Cultivar	Plant form originating in cultivation.
Cutting	Vegetative plant part capable of producing identical plant.
Deciduous	Plants that lose leaves at maturity in certain seasons.
Diploid	Orchid with the normal number of chromosomes.
Division	The means by which a single cultivar is divided into two or more plants.
Dormant	Resting, a period of inactivity when plants grow less or not at all.
Dorsal	Pertaining to the back or outer surface.
Epiphyte	A plant that grows on another plant but is not a parasite, as it obtains nourishment from the air.
Eye	The bud of a growth.
Family	A group of related genera.
Force	To make a plant grow or bloom ahead of its natural season.
Gene	The unit of inheritance, located at a specific site on a chromosome.
Genetics	The study of heredity and variation.
Genus	A subdivision of a family, consisting of one or more species that show similar characteristics and appear to have a common ancestry.
Germination	Process of seed sprouting.
Grex	A grex name is the named cross between two different orchids.

Habitat The locality in which a plant normally grows.

Hirsute Pubescent, the hairs being coarse and stiff.

Hybrid The offspring resulting from the cross between two different species or hybrids.

Indigenous Native; not introduced.

Inflorescence The flowering part of a plant.

Intergeneric Between or among two or more genera.

Internode The part of a stem between two nodes.

Keel A projecting ridge.

Keiki A plantlet produced as an offset or offshoot from another plant, a Hawaiian term used by orchidists.

Labellum The lip, or modified petal of an orchid flower.

Lateral Of or pertaining to the side of an organ.

Lead A new vegetative growth.

Leaflet Segment of a compound leaf.

Leafmold Decayed or decomposed leaves, useful in potting mixes.

Linear Long and narrow, with parallel margins.

Lip The labellum, usually quite different from the other two petals.

Lithophyte A plant that grows on rocks.

Mericlone A plant produced by meristem culture.

Meristem Vegetative propagation of plants.

Monopodial Growing only from the apex of the plant.

Mutation A departure from the parent type; a sport.

Natural hybrid A hybrid produced by chance in the wild.

Node   A joint on a stem where a bud or leaf is attached.

Nomenclature   A system of names or naming.

Offset   A plantlet that may form at the base of an orchid, on the stem, pseudobulb, or inflorescence.

Parasite   A plant that lives on and derives part or all of its nourishment from another plant.

Petal   One of the three inner segments of an orchid flower, which is not modified to form the lip.

Petiole   Supporting stalk of a leaf.

Pinnate   Leaf form, like a feather, with sections arranged along the side of the leaf stalk.

Pistil   The seed-bearing organ of a flower, consisting of the ovary, stigma, and style.

Plicate   Pleated or folded like a fan.

Pollen   The fertilizing grains borne by the anther.

Pollination   The transfer of pollen from the anther to the stigma.

Polyploid   Containing one or more additional sets of chromosomes beyond the normal diploid number.

Potbound   Condition of a plant when a mat of roots fills the container.

Protocorm   A tuberlike structure formed in the early stages of a plant's development.

Psuedobulb   The thickened portion of a stem, but not a true bulb.

Quadrigeneric   Pertaining to four genera.

Raceme   A simple inflorescence of stalked flowers.

Rhizome   A root-bearing horizontal stem, which, in orchids, usually lies on or just beneath the ground surface.

Rosette   A cluster of leaves arranged around a short stem.

Saccate	Pouched or baglike.
Scape	A flower stalk without leaves, arising directly from the ground.
Self-pollination	The pollination of a flower by its own pollen.
Semiterete	Semicircular in cross-section; semicylindrical.
Sepal	One of the three outer segments of an orchid flower.
Sheath	A tubular envelope protecting the developing buds.
Species	A group of plants sharing one or more common characteristics.
Sphagnum moss	Bog material dried and used alone as a planting medium or in a mixture.
Spike	A flower stem.
Sport	A deviation from the usual form; a mutation.
Spur	A hollow tubular extension of the lip.
Stamen	The male organ of a flower, bearing the pollen.
Stigma	The part of the pistil that is receptive to the pollen.
Stolon	Creeping horizontal stem usually producing a new plant at the tip.
Style	The part of the pistil bearing the stigma.
Succulent	Type of plant that stores moisture in stems or leaves.
Symbiosis	The close association of dissimilar organisms, with benefit to both.
Sympodial	A form of growth in which each new shoot, arising from the rhizome of the previous growth, is a complete plant in itself.
Taxonomist	Scientific specialist concerned with plant names.
Terete	Circular in cross-section; cylindrical.

Terrestrial Growing in or on the ground.

Tetraploid Plant cells with four times the normal number of chromosomes, compared to common species having a diploid number of chromosomes.

Transpiration The loss of water from the plant tissue by evaporation.

Tribe A group of related genera.

Trigeneric Pertaining to three genera.

Tuber A thickened, normally underground stem.

Umbel Flat or ball-shaped flower cluster.

Unifoliate Having one leaf.

Unilateral Arranged only on one side.

Unisexual Having flowers of one sex only.

Vandaceous Refers to Vanda genera and to plants that have a monopodial type of growth.

Vegetative propagation The increasing of a particular plant by division.

Virus An infectious agent that increases in living cells, causing disease.

Appendix 1
United States Orchid Suppliers

Alberts & Merkel Bros., Inc.
2210 South Federal Highway
Boynton Beach, FL 33435
Orchid list: $1
Free to member of an orchid society

The Angraecum House
P.O. Box 976
Grass Valley, CA 95945
African and Madagascan species
Write for information

Arm-Roy
3376 Foothill Road
P.O. Box 385
Carpinteria, CA 93013
Species, hybrids

Bates Orchids, Inc.
7911 U.S. Highway 301
Ellenton, FL 33532-3599
Species

John Berryman Orchids
1393 U.S. Route 17
Tabb, VA 23602
Cattleyas, Phalaenopses

Blueberry Hill Orchids
12 Charles Street
Lexington, MA 02173
Phalaenopses
Lists available

Bo-Mar Orchids
P.O. Box 6713
San Bernardino, CA 92412
Cattleyas
Seedling and flask list: $1

Boulder Valley Orchids
240 Second Avenue
P.O. Box 45
Niwot, CO 80544
Paphiopedilums

Carmela Orchids,Inc.
P.O. Box H
Hakalau,HI 96710
Cattleyas, Phalaenopses
Free price list

Carter & Holmes, Inc.
#1 Old Mendenhall Road
P.O. Box 668
Newberry, SC 29108
Free list

La Casa Verde
35601 SW 192d Avenue
Homestead, FL 33034
All types of orchids
Free price list

Chester Hills Orchids
962 Catfish Lane
Pottstown, PA 19464
Phalaenopses
Write for lists

Chula Orchids
230 Chula Vista Street
Chula Vista, CA 92010
Hybrids, species
Free lists

Clark Day Orchids
1911 South Bloomfield
Cerritos, CA 90701
Odontoglossums, Paphiopedilums

Crystal Orchids
608 Bob White Road
Wayne, PA 19087
Paphiopedilum hybrids

Drago Orchid Corp.
4601 SW 127th Avenue
Miami, FL 33175
Cattleya species
Free list

E-Z Orchids
Box 209
Berwyn, PA 19312
Phalaenopses, Cattleyas
Free lists

Evon Orchids
Box 17396
San Diego, CA 92117
Seedlings, mature plants
Free list

John Ewing Orchids, Inc.
P.O. Box 384
Aptos, CA 95003
Phalaenopses
Free catalog

Exotics Hawaii Limited
1344 Hoakoa Place
Honolulu, HI 96821
Cattleyas, Dendrobiums, Vandas,
    Oncidiums, and other orchids
No catalogs or price list available;
    send self-addressed stamped
    envelope for further inquiry

Farnsworth Orchids
606 North Lanikai Place
Haiku, Maui, HI 96708
Ascocendas
List on request

Fennell's Orchid Jungle
26715 SW 157th Avenue
Homestead, FL 33031
Cattleyas

Finck Floral Co.
9849-A Kimker Lane
St. Louis, MO 63127-1599
Cattleyas, species orchids
Free lists on request

Fordyce Orchids
7259 Tina Place
Dublin, CA 94568
Miniature Cattleyas
By appointment

Fort Caroline Orchids
13142 Fort Caroline Road
Jacksonville, FL 32225
Species, Brassias, hybrids

The Garden District
6525 Washington Street
Vintage 1870
Youthville, CA 94599
All kinds of orchids
No lists or catalog

Great Lakes Orchids
28805 Pennsylvania Road
Romulus, MI 48174
Species
Write for list

Hartmann's Orchid Lab
424 NE 28th Road
Boca Raton, FL 33431
Phalaenopses

Spencer M. Howard Orchid
    Imports
11802 Huston Street
North Hollywood, CA 91607
Species
Send self-addressed stamped
    envelope for free price list

Huan Bui Orchids, Inc.
6900 SW 102d Avenue
Miami, FL 33173
Seedlings and clones
Catalog: $2

Islander Delights Orchids
14568 Twin Peaks Road
Poway, CA 92064
Oncidiums, Dendrobiums, Vandas
Free list

J. E. M. Orchids
4996 NE Fourth Avenue
Boca Raton, FL 33431
Mini Cattleyas, Oncidium
   intergenerics

J & L Orchids
20 Sherwood Road
Easton, CT 06612
All kinds of orchids
Write for free catalog

Jemmco Flowers
Box 23
St. George, SC 29477
Cattleya seedlings

Jenetta Nursery
3724 School Road
P.O. Box 298
Fresno, TX 77545
Different varieties

Robert Jones' Mt. Madonna Orchids
126 Hughes Road
Watsonville, CA 95076
Paphiopedilum
Lists available

Jones & Scully, Inc.
2200 NW 33d Avenue
Miami, FL 33142
Catalog: $5

Kaoru Oka Orchids
1346 Wilhelmina Rise
Honolulu, HI 96816
Cattleyas
Free list

Kensington Orchids, Inc.
3301 Plyers Mill Road
Kensington, MD 20795
Cattleyas; species

Arnold J. Klemm, grower
2 E. Algonquin Road
Arlington Heights, IL 60005
Phalaenopses
Free list

Krull-Smith Orchids
Ponkan Road, Route 3, Box 18A
Apopka, FL 32703
Cattleyas, Phalaenopses

Lauralin Orchids
Route 6, Box 1290B
Mocksville, NC 27028
Miniatures, species
List on request

Laurel Orchids
18205 SW 157th Avenue
Miami, FL 33187
Species, seedlings
Free catalog

Laurelwood Orchids, Inc.
778 Old White Horse Pike
Waterford, NJ 08089
Pots and seedlings

Lines Orchids
1823 Taft Highway
Signal Mountain, TN 37377
Seedlings and flowering plants
No catalog

Lynette Greenhouses
4345 Rogers Lake Road
Kannapolis, NC 28081
Cattleyas

Madcap Orchids
Route 29, Box 391-UU
Fort Myers, FL 33905
Dendrobiums

Maka Koa Corporation
Box 411 .
Haleiwa, HI 96712
Cattleyas

Ann Mann
Route 3, Box 202
Orlando, FL 32811
Ascocendas, Vandas
Catalog

Maxwell Company
P.O. Box 13141
Fresno, CA 93794
Hybrids
Lists available

McClains' Orchid Range
6237 Blanding Boulevard
Jacksonville, FL 32244
Miniature and small growing plants

Rod McLellan Co.
1450 El Camino Real
San Francisco, CA 94080
Oncidiums, Cattleyas, Cymbidiums
Catalog: 50¢

Merryl's
Div. of Miah, Inc.
6660 Busch Boulevard
Columbus, OH 43229
Miniature orchids
Send self-addressed stamped
   envelope for free list

Mobile Bay Orchids
Route 1, Box 166-D
Mobile, AL 36605
Various orchids
Write for free list

Paul A. Mulcey
Orchid Grower
R.D. 2
Dallas, PA 18612
Paphiopedilums

Muses' Orchids
3710 North Orchid Drive
Haines City, FL 33844
Seedlings to mature plants
Free list

Oak Hill Gardens
P.O. Box 25
Dundee, IL 60118
Species, hybrids
Free catalog

Oakmont Orchids
P.O. Box 142
Pelham, AL 35124
Cymbidiums and other orchids
Catalog

Okika Ltd. Orchid Growers
1431 La Loma Drive
Nipomo, CA 93444
Miltonias, Odontoglossums

The Orchid Center
Highway 17, Box 1116
Arcadia, FL 33821
Free catalog

The Orchid House
1699 Sage Avenue
Los Osos, CA 93402
Phalaenopses
No lists

Orchid Species Specialties
P.O. Box 1003
Arcadia, CA 91006
Species
List: $1

Orchid World International, Inc.
11295 SW 93d Street
Miami, FL 33176
Cattleyas, Oncidiums, and others

Orchids Bountiful
826 West 3800 South
Bountiful, UT 84010
Species

Orchids by Hausermann, Inc.
2N134 Addison Road
Villa Park, IL 60181
All orchids

Orchids Ltd.
407 E. Carson Street
Carson, CA 90745
Jungle-collected plants

Owens Orchids
P.O. Box 365
Pisgah Forest, NC 28768
Miniature and compact Cattleyas

Paradise of Orchids
1608 Waterline Road
Bradenton, FL 34202
Vandaceous orchid specialists

Pearl Harbor Orchids
99-007 Kealakaha Drive
Aiea, HI 96701

Peninsula Hybrids
635 Marion Avenue
Palo Alto, CA 94301
Hybrids and species

Penn Valley Orchids
239 Old Gulph Road
Wynnewood, PA 19096
Paphiopedilum
Send self-addressed stamped
    envelope for lists; catalog: $2

Quality Orchids
P.O. Box 4472
Hialeah, FL 33014
Send for list

R. F. Orchids
28100 SW 182d Avenue
Homestead, FL 33030
Vandas, Ascocendas
List available

J. R. Rands Orchids
15322 Mulholland Drive
Los Angeles, CA 90077
Cattleyas, species

Joseph R. Redlinger Orchids
9236 SW 57th Avenue
Miami, FL 33156
Cattleyas

Ridgeway Orchid Gardens
2467 Ridgeway Drive
National City, CA 92050
Cymbidium, Phalaenopses

Riverbend Orchids
Route 1, Box 590E
Biloxi, MS 39532
Hybrids
Free list available

Riverview Orchids Inc.
1860 Parkway Road
East Liverpool, OH 43920
Cymbidiums

Rubin In Orchids
15200 SW 46th Street
Miami, FL 33175
Meristems
List on request

Santa Barbara Orchid Estate
1250 Orchid Drive
Santa Barbara, CA 93111
Miltonias, Cymbidiums, and other
orchids

Sea Breeze Orchids, Inc.
P.O. Box 1416
Bayville, NY 11709
Sophronitis
Free catalog

Sea God Nurseries
P.O. Box 678
Geyersville, CA 95441
Cattleya seedlings
Free list

Seagulls Landing Orchids
P.O. Box 388
Glen Head, NY 11545
Miniature Cattleyas
Free catalog

Stewart Orchids, Inc.
1212 E. Las Tunas Drive
P.O. Box 307
San Gabriel, CA 91778
Cattleyas, Cymbidiums, and
miniature Cattleyas
Lists available

Su-An Nursery
58 Kirklees Road
Pittsford, NY 14534
Phalaenopses and Cattleyas only
Free catalog on request

Sunswept Laboratories
P.O. Box 1913
Studio City, CA 91604
Phalaenopses, orchid seed sowing,
and micropropagation

Tammany Tropicals
Unlimited, Inc.
760 North Causeway Boulevard
Mandeville, LA 70448
Phalaenopses
Send self-addressed stamped
envelope for current price list

Taylor Orchids
P.O. Box 267
Monroe, MI 48161
Paphiopedilum and other orchids

Tonkin's Orchids, Inc.
119 St. Alban's Road
Kensington, CA 94708
Paphiopedilums

Trymwood Orchids
2500 Rockdell Street
La Crescenta, CA 91214
Colored Cattleyas
Flask list available

J. Milton Warne
260 Jack Lane
Honolulu, HI 96817
Hybrids
No catalog

Ken West Orchids
P.O. Box 1332
Pahoa, HI 96778

Wilk Orchid Specialties
P.O. Box 1177
Kaneohe, HI 96744
Assorted orchids of many kinds
No catalog

Yamamoto Dendrobiums Hawaii
P.O. Box 235
Mountain View, HI 96771
Dendrobiums
Color catalog: $2

Yardley Orchids
1225 Madison Drive
Yardley, PA 19067
Phalaenopses

Zuma Canyon Orchids, Inc.
5949 Bonsall Drive
Malibu, CA 90265
Phalaenopses
Free list on request

Appendix 2
British Orchid Suppliers

Bardfield Orchids
Great Bardfield
Braintree, Essex CM7 4RZ
Open Saturdays & Mondays only

Burnham Nurseries Ltd.
Orchid Avenue
Kingsteignton
Newton Abbot, Devon TQ12 3HG
Mail order; wholesale

Ivens Orchids Ltd.
St. Albans Road
Sandridge, Herts. AL4 9LB
Wholesale

A. J. Keeling & Son
Grange Nurseries
Westgate Hill
Bradford, Yorks.

Keith Andrew Orchids Ltd.
Plush
Dorchester, Dorset DT2 7RH
Mail order; wholesale

Lipanda Orchids
The Vandas
Sidbury
Bridgnorth, Shropshire WV16 6PY
Mail order; wholesale

Mansell & Hatcher Ltd.
Cragg Wood Nurseries
Rawdon
Leeds LS19 6LQ
Mail order; wholesale

McBeans Orchids Ltd.
Cooksbridge
Lewes, Sussex
Mail order; wholesale

Ratcliffe Orchids Ltd.
Chilton
Didcot, Oxon OX11 ORT
Mail order; wholesale

Royden Orchids
Perks Lane
Prestwood
Great Missenden, Bucks

St. Dunstan's Nursery
Ham Street
Baltonsborough
Glastonbury, Somerset

David Stead Orchids
Leeds Road Nurseries
Lofthouse
Wakefield, West Yorks.

Stonehurst Orchid Nursery
Ardingly, Sussex

Wellbank Orchids
Pardon
Oakley, Hants. RG23 7DY
Mail order

Wyld Court Orchids
Hampstead Norreys
Newbury, Berks.
Mail order

All these firms sell to the public, and all will gladly give help and advice, but visitors should telephone before arrival to ensure proper attention. The British Orchid Growers Association holds its annual show every March at the Royal Horticular Society Hall, Vincent Square, Westminster, London.

Appendix 3
International Orchid Suppliers

The Bangkrabue Nursery
174 Ruam Chit Lane
Amnuai Songkhram Road
P.O. Box 3-150
Bangkok 3, Thailand 10 300
Orchids of Thailand
Free list

Caribe Orchid Growers
P.O. Box 26
Carolina, Puerto Rico 00628
Species

Charles Island Gardens
Box 91471
West Vancouver, B.C.
Canada, V7V 3P2
Miniature Cymbidiums

Green Orchids Company
P.O. Box 7-587
Taipei, Taiwan, R.O.C.
Cattleyas

Kabukiran Orchids
81 Maginoo Street
P.O. Box 7744 ADC
Quezon City, Philippines
Philippine orchids
List: $1

E. G. Kamm
Valle de Angeles, F.M.
Honduras
Orchid species
Free price list

Marcel Lecoufle
5, rue de Paris
94470 Boissy-St. Léger, France
Orchids
Catalog and list on request

Nurseryman's Haven
Kalimpong 734301, India
Indo-Burmese and Himalayan
    orchids
Free list

Sukhakul Nursery
15 Klahom Lane
P.O. Box 3-97
Bangkrabue
Bangkok 3, Thailand
Thai orchid species
Free list

T. Orchids
77/3 Chaengwattana Road
(Rim Klong Prapa)
Pak-kred Nonthaburi, Thailand
P.O. Box 21-19
Bangkok, Thailand
Vandas, Ascocendas, Dendrobiums
Catalog and price list: $5

Vacherot & Lecoufle
"La Tuilerie"
30 rue de Valenton, BP8
94470 Boissy-St-Léger, France
Orchids from all genera
Color catalog: $2

Appendix 4
Equipment Suppliers and Book Dealers

The Backdoor Pottery
P.O. Box 981
Ingram, TX 78025
Orchid pots

Clarel Laboratories, Inc.
513 Grove
Deerfield, IL 60015
Orchid food
Free catalog

Day's
4725 NW 36th Avenue
Miami, FL 33142
Tier plant benches
Free brochures

Environmental Concepts
710 NW 57th Street
Fort Lauderdale, FL 33309
Light-intensity meter

Finck Floral Co.
9849-A Kimker Lane
St. Louis, MO 63127
Orchid food

Hydrofarm
150 Bellam Boulevard
Suite 300-AO
San Rafael, CA 94901
Lighting supplies
Free catalog

Idle Hours Orchids
905 SW Coconut Drive
Fort Lauderdale, FL 33315
Servo orchid potting mix

Indoor Gardening Supplies
P.O. Box 40567A0
Detroit, MI 48240
Plant stands, lamps, accessories
Free catalog

Keiki Grow
Dr. James D. Brasch
Box 354, McMaster University
Hamilton, Ontario L8S 1C0 Canada
Plant hormones

B. D. Lynn
1438 West Valerio Street
Santa Barbara, CA 93101
Orchids in gold (jewelry)

Maryland Cork Co., Inc.
P.O. Box 126
Elkton, MD
Cork nuggets

Don Mattern
267 Filbert Street
San Francisco, CA 94133
Humidifiers for greenhouses

McQuerry Orchid Books
Mary Noble McQuerry
5700 West Salerno Road
Jacksonville, FL 32244
Rare, old, and new books

Ofiduca International, Inc.
P.O. Box 161302
Miami, FL 33116
Potting mediums
Free catalog

Orchid Art Gallery
1765 Victory Boulevard
Staten Island, NY 10314
Indoor greenhouses

Orchid Lovers Sales Directory &
  Guide to Regional Sources
P.O. Box 17125
Rochester, NY 14617
Regional guidebook to orchid
  societies
Write for price

Pacific Coast Greenhouse Mfg. Co.
8360 Industrial Avenue
Cotati, CA 94928
Humidifiers
Free brochures and price list

Spiral Filtration, Inc.
747 North Twin Oaks Valley Road
  #13
San Marcos, CA 92069
Water-purification system
Catalog: $5

F.M.S. Orchids
"The Homestead"
High Street
Stockbridge, Hants.
Hobby flasks

H.A.G.A.
100 Pullar Road
Barnet, Herts.
Heating systems for orchid-growing

H. G. Hees
99A Kiln Ride
Wokingham, Berks. RG11 3PD
Books, composts, culture media,
  plant food, equipment

Tropical Plant Products, Inc.
P.O. Box 7754
Orlando, FL 32854
Tree fern products, potting
  mediums, fertilizers, wire goods
Free catalog

Twin Oaks Books
4343 Causeway Drive
Lowell, MI 49331
Orchid books; vast selection

Yonah Manufacturing Co.
P.O. Box 280 AO
Cornelia, GA 30531
Shade cloth
Free informational kit

Silvaperl Products Ltd.
P.O. Box 8
Harrogate, North Yorks. HG2 8JW
Growing media

C. H. Whitehouse Ltd.
Buckhurst Works
Frant, Sussex TN3 9BN
All-cedar orchid houses; ventilation
  and heating equipment

Appendix 5
Orchid Societies and Periodicals

Membership in any society listed below brings with it the society's valuable publication.

The American Orchid Society
The American Orchid Society Bulletin
6000 South Olive Street
West Palm Beach, FL 33405
  $20/yr., published monthly

Cymbidium Society of America
The Orchid Advocate
5902 Via Real
Carpinteria, CA 93013
  $12.50/yr., published bimonthly

The Orchid Digest Corporation
The Orchid Digest
c/o Mrs. Norman H. Atkinson
P.O. Box 916
Carmichael, CA 95609-0916
  $18/yr., published bimonthly

South Florida Orchid Society
The Florida Orchidist
13300 SW 111th Avenue
Miami, FL 33176
  $12/yr., published quarterly

Australian Orchid Review
P.O. Box 60
Sydney Mail Exchange, Australia
  2012
  published quarterly

The Orchid Review
5 Orchid Avenue, Kingsteignton
Newton Abbot, Devon TQ12 3HG
  England
  published monthly

South African Orchid Journal
c/o Hugh Rogers, editor
10 Somers Road
Clarendon
Pietermaritzburg 3201, South Africa
  published quarterly

Bibliography

AMES, BLANCHE. *Drawings of Florida Orchids*. 2d ed. Explanatory Notes by Oakes Ames. Cambridge, Mass.: Botanical Museum of Harvard University, 1959.

————, AND DONOVAN S. CORRELL. *Orchids of Guatemala*. Chicago: Field Museum of Natural History, 1952–53. (Fieldiana: Botany, Vol. 26, Nos. 1 and 2.) Supplement by Correll, 1966. 2 vols., 726 pages.

BAILEY, LIBERTY HYDE. *Standard Cyclopedia of Horticulture*. Popular ed. New York: Macmillan, 1935. 3 vols., 3,639 pages.

BLOWERS, JOHN W. *Pictorial Orchid Growing*. Maidstone, Kent, England: John W. Blowers, 96 Marion Crescent, 1966. 128 pages.

BOYLE, FREDERICK. *The Culture of Greenhouse Orchids: Old System and New*. London: 1902.

BOYLE, LOUIS M. *Growing Cymbidium Orchids and Other Flowers*. Ojai, Calif.: El Rancho Rinconada, 1953. 520 pages.

CADY, LEO, AND T. ROTHERHAM. *Australian Orchids in Color*. Sydney: Reed, 1970. 50 text pages, 107 color plates.

CHITTENDEN, FRED J. *Dictionary of Gardening*. 4 vols. Oxford: Clarendon Press, 1951, 1956, 1965.

CORRELL, DONOVAN S. *Native Orchids of North America, North of Mexico*. New York: Ronald, 1950. 400 pages.

COX, J. M. *Cultural Table of Orchidaceous Plants*. Sydney: Shepherd, 1946.

CRAIGHEAD, FRANK S. *Orchids and Other Air Plants of the Everglades National Park*. Coral Gables, Fla.: University of Miami Press, 1963. 125 pages.

CURTIS, CHARLES H. *Orchids: Their Description and Cultivation*. London: Putnam, 1950. 274 pages.

DARWIN, CHARLES. *The Various Contrivances by Which Orchids Are Fertilised by Insects*. New York: Appleton, 1892; London: Murray, 1904.

DAVIS, REG. S., AND MONA LISA STEINER. *Philippine Orchids*. New York: William Frederick Press, 1952. 270 pages.

DOCKRILL, A. W. *Australian Indigenous Orchids*. Sydney: 1969. 825 pages.

DODSON, CALAWAY H., AND ROBERT J. GILLESPIE. *The History of the Orchids*. Nashville, Tenn.: Mid-America Orchid Congress, 1967. 158 pages.

DUNSTERVILLE, G. C. K. *Introduction to the World of Orchids*. Garden City, N.Y.: Doubleday, 1964. 104 pages.

FENNELL, T. A., JR. *Orchids for Home and Garden*. New York: Rinehart, 1956. Rev. ed., 1959.

GARRARD, JEANNE. *Growing Orchids for Pleasure*. South Brunswick, N.J.: Barnes, 1966. 302 pages.

GHOSE, B. N. *Beautiful Indian Orchids*. Darjeeling: Ghose, 1959. 2d ed., 1969. 155 pages.

GILBERT, P. A. *Orchids: Their Culture and Classification*. Sydney: Shepherd, 1951. 252 pages.

GRAF, ALFRED BYRD. *Exotica 3: Pictorial Cyclopedia of Exotic Plants*. Rutherford, N.J.: Roehrs, 1963. 1,828 pages, 901 illustrations and descriptions of orchids.

GRUBB, ROY, AND ANN GRUBB. *Selected Orchidaceous Plants*. Parts 1-3. Caterham, Surrey: Roy and Ann Grubb, 62 Chaldon Common Road, 1961–63. Drawn and hand-printed by the authors.

HARVARD UNIVERSITY BOTANICAL MUSEUM LEAFLETS. By subscription, or available separately from the American Orchid Society, 6000 South Olive Street, West Palm Beach, Fla. 33405.

HAWKES, ALEX D. *Encyclopaedia of Cultivated Orchids*. London: Faber and Faber, 1965. 602 pages.

———. *Orchids: Their Botany and Culture*. New York: Harper & Row, 1961. 297 pages.

HOGG, BRUCE. *Orchids: Their Culture*. Melbourne and Sydney: Cassell, 1957. 139 pages.

HOOKER, SIR JOSEPH DALTON. *A Century of Orchidaceous Plants*. London: Reeve & Benham, 1851. 78 pages.

KRAMER, JACK. *Growing Orchids at Your Windows*. New York: Van Nostrand, 1963. 151 pages.

———, AND ROY CRAFTON. *Miniature Orchids to Grow and Show*. New York: Norton, 1981. 160 pages.

KUPPER, WALTER, AND WALTER LINSENMAIER. *Orchidées*. Zurich: Service d'Images Silva, c. 1955. *Orchids*. Edinburgh: Nelson, 1961. 128 pages. 100 color plates.

LECOUFLE, MARCEL, AND HENRI ROSE. *Orchids*. London: Crosby, Lockwood, 1957. 112 pages.

LOGAN, HARRY B., AND LLOYD C. COOPER. *Orchids Are Easy to Grow*. Chicago: Ziff-Davis, 1949. 312 pages.

MOULEN, FRED. *Orchids in Australia*. Sydney: Australia Edita, 1958. 148 pages, 100 color figures.

NOBLE, MARY. *You Can Grow Cattleya Orchids*. Jacksonville, Fla.: Mary Noble, 3003 Riverside Avenue, 1968. 148 pages.

OCA, RAFAEL MONTES DE. *Hummingbirds and Orchids of Mexico*. Mexico: Fournier, 1963. 158 pages, reproductions of watercolor paintings.

OSORIO, LUIS F. *Orguideas colombianas*. (*Colombian Orchids*). Medellin: Bedout, 1941. 106 leaves. Text in Spanish and English.

RICHTER, WALTER. *Die Schönsten aber sind Orchideen*. Radebeul: Neumann, 1958. Translated and revised as *The Orchid World*. New York: Dutton, 1965. 280 pages, 64 color plates.

RITTERSHAUSEN, P. R. C. *Successful Orchid Culture*. London: Collingridge; New York: Transatlantic Arts, 1953. 136 pages.

SANDER, DAVID. *Orchids and Their Cultivation*. Rev. ed. London: Blandford, 1962. 183 pages.

SANDER, FRED. *Reichenbachia: Orchids Illustrated and Described*. 4 vols. London, 1888-94. The plates are now collectors' items.

SANDER & SONS. *Complete List of Orchid Hybrids*. St. Albans, Herts.: Sander, 1946. Addenda, 3 vols., 1946-48, 1949-51, 1952-54.

————. *One-Table List of Orchid Hybrids, 1946-60*. 2 vols. St. Albans, Herts.: Sander, 1961. Addenda, 1963, 1966.

————. *Sander's Orchid Guide*. Rev. ed. St. Albans, Herts.: Sanders, 1927. 451 pages.

Sander's List of Orchid Hybrids. London: Royal Horticultural Society. Addenda, 1961-70, 1971-75, 1976-80. Also available from the American Orchid Society, 6000 South Olive Street, West Palm Beach, Fla. 33405.

SCHELPE, E. A. C. L. E. *An Introduction to the South African Orchids*. London: Macdonald, 1966. 109 pages.

SCHWEINFURTH, CHARLES. *Orchids of Peru*. 4 vols. Chicago: Field Museum of Natural History, 1958-61. (Fieldiana: Botany, Vol. 30, Nos. 1-4.) 1,005 pages.

SUMMERHAYES, V. S. *Wild Orchids of Britain*. London: Collins, 1951. 366 pages.

THOMALE, HANS. *Die Orchideen*. Ludwigsburg: Ulmer, 1954. Text in German. 189 pages.

VEITCH, JAMES & SONS. *A Manual of Orchidaceous Plants*. 4 vols. Reprint. Amsterdam: Ashler, 1963.

WATKINS, JOHN V. *ABC of Orchid Growing*. 3d ed. Englewood Cliffs, N.J.: Prentice-Hall, 1956. 190 pages.

WATSON, WILLIAM AND H. J. CHAPMAN. *Orchids: Their Culture and Management*. Rev. ed. London: Gill, 1903.

WHITE, E. A. *American Orchid Culture*. Rev. ed. New York: De La Mare, 1942.

WILLIAMS, B. S. *The Orchid Grower's Manual*. 7th ed., rev. by Henry Williams, 1894. Reprinted. Hitchin, Herts. England: Wheldon & Wesley, 1960.

WILLIAMS, JOHN G., AND ANDREW E. WILLIAMS. *Field Guide to Orchids of North America*. New York: Universe Books, 1983. Illustrated by Norman Arlott. 144 pages.

WILLIAMS, LOUIS O. *The Orchidaceae of Mexico*. Tegucigalpa, Honduras: Escuela Agricola Panamericana, 1952. (Cieba, Vol. 2, in 4 parts.)

WITHNER, CARL L. *The Orchids: A Scientific Survey*. New York: Ronald, 1959. 648 pages.

WRIGHT, N. PELHAM. *Orquideas de Mexico*. Mexico, D.F.: La Prensa Médica Mexicana, 1958. Bilingual text. 120 pages.

Index